PARIS

D0115665

Urban Crayon Paris © April 2008 by **Sheridan Becker and Kim Barrington Narisetti**
Contributor: **Erszi Deàk**
Photographs: **Sheridan Becker and Michel Bries**
Graphic Design: **Frederic Selis** (frederic.selis@skynet.be)
Printed in India – **Creative Design Studio**, G-21, Gail No.3, Ganga Vihar, New Delhi

Send queries to
Publisher: Urban Crayon Press
3020 Lost Creek Blvd.
Laurel, Md. 20724

Although the authors and publisher try to make the information as accurate as possible, we accept
no responsibility for any loss, injury, or inconvenience sustained by anyone using this book.

First Edition

Library of Congress Control Number: 2007943293

Reinforced binding

ISBN 978-0-9795534-0-0

Visit us at **www.urbancrayonpress.com** or email **urbancrayonpress@aol.com** to tell us how to make
the second edition even better. If we use a tip sent in by you, you'll get an urban crayon fun pack.

PARIS – BONJOUR, BABY!

Given the number of skinny women roaming "the City of light" in little black dresses and heels, busily discussing sartre and the Delaunays, an average mother isn't likely to think of Paris as the top choice for a family vacation. It tops the list for a romantic weekend, but the thought of a weeklong jaunt would probably get a firm non. And while the narrow streets and general lack of ramps and elevators may indeed seem stroller-unfriendly, this city of "perspectives" and gastronomy is home to 2.15 million humans (many of whom are children) and can in fact lend itself to be a memorable vacation for the kids. More people visit Paris (about 44 million annually) than any other city in the world. And many of those visitors are kids. For all its style and sophistication, Paris will always be a big hit for children of all ages because of its hidden paths, city gardens, and gruesome gargoyles to its majestic monuments. The city is a storybook setting waiting to be read by both parent and child. It is truly a walking city with few lifts, so babies and toddlers will be better off in backpacks than buggies. But before we take the family on this magnificent journey through Paris, we're going to get the important stuff out of the way. *Bon voyage.*

VISAS

U.S. citizens and those of Canada, New Zealand, Norway and EU countries do not need a visa to enter France, and can stay for up to 90 days. Visitors from other countries must obtain a visa before arrival in France from the French Consulate in their home country.

EMBASSIES IN PARIS

> **Australia,** 4 rue Jean Rey, 15ᵉ
  TᴇL: 33 1 40 593 300
> **Canada,** 35 av Montaigne, 8ᵉ
  TᴇL: 33 1 44 432 900
> **Israel,** 3 rue Rabelais, 8ᵉ
  TᴇL: 33 1 40 765 500
> **Japan,** 7 av Hoche, 8ᵉ
  TᴇL: 33 1 48 886 200
> **Saudi Arabia,**
  4 bis rue de Franqueville, 16ᵉ
  Fax: 33 1 40 501 626
> **South Africa,** 59 quai d'Orsay, 7ᵉ
  TᴇL: 33 1 45 559 237
> **United Kingdom,**
  35 rue du fbg St Honoré, 8ᵉ
  TᴇL: 33 1 44 513 100
> **United States,** 2 av Gabriel, 8ᵉ
  TᴇL: 33 1 43 122 222

WEATHER

Average temperature per season

	Mᴀxɪᴍᴜᴍ	Mɪɴɪᴍᴜᴍ
Jan. to March	59F/15°c	54F/12°c
March to May	70F/21°c	54F/12°c
June to August	83F/28°c	57F/14°c
Sept. to Nov.	61F/16°c	43F/6°c

TELEPHONE

To call Paris from abroad: Dial 00, then the access code for France (33) , followed by 1, then the eight-digit phone number.
To call abroad from Paris: 001 followed by the area code for the U.S., and 00 followed by the country code, then the phone number for other countries.
To reach a local number in Paris: Direct-dial the 10-digit phone number. Local numbers in Paris and Ile de France always begin with the 01.
Directory assistance: 118.
Directory assistance in English: 08 00 364 775.
Horloge parlante (time): 36 99. Unless your mobile phone is GSM enabled, it's best to purchase a pre-paid phone card sold in various denominations from a *magasin* (book/magazine shop).

EMERGENCY NUMBERS

Ambulance: TᴇL 15
Fire: TᴇL 18
Police: TᴇL 17 (the equivalent of '911' in the U.S.). From a cell phone, dial 112.

24-HOUR PHONE INFORMATION SERVICE IN ENGLISH

Offers complete tourist information for Paris and surrounding areas. It lists all the best restaurants, hotels, museums and events. In partnership with the Regional Tourist Board, it is accessible by land line and mobile phones.

Tel: 118247

www.118247.fr

RATES INCLUDING TAX: €1.35 A CALL PLUS 34 CENTS A MINUTE.

24-HOUR BABY-SITTING

Expect to pay €5-15 an hour for baby-sitting, depending on the service. The going rate for agencies is in the €7-12 range. The hourly rate for a baby-sitter is about €6-8. Be prepared to pay at least double (that's at least €15 an hour, or more) if you need a sitter on French national holidays. It is also customary to pay the baby-sitter for a taxi after midnight.

> Allo! Maman Poule
Tel 01 45 209 696
> Ave Pro Sitting
Tel: 01 44 379 111
www.prositting.com

OTHER BABY-SITTING SERVICES

> 1, 2, 3 Soleil
Tel: 01 43 574 453
> Ababa
Tel: 01 45 494 646
> Maman Kid Service
Tel: 01 47 660 052
> Baby-sitting service
Tel: 01 46 375 124

HOSPITALS

> American Hospital in Paris
63 blvd Victor Hugo
Neuilly-sur-Seine
Tel: 01 46 612 525
www.american-hospital.org
MÉTRO: CHARLES DE GAULLE
> Franco-British Hospital
3 rue Barbes, Levallois-Perret
Tel: 01 46 392 222
www.british-hospital.org.

HOUSE CALLS

S.O.S. Médecins
Tel: 01 47 077 777 AND REQUEST AN ENGLISH-SPEAKING DOCTOR. WAIT TIME IS ABOUT AN HOUR. COST: €60 DURING THE DAY AND €90 AT NIGHT.
www.sosmedecins.fr

24-HOUR DENTIST

Hôpital Franco-Britannique (Hertford British Hospital)
3 rue Barbes, Levallois-Perret
Tel: 01 46 392 222
www.british-hospital.org

SOS Dentaire
Address: 87 blvd Port-Royal, 13ᵉ
Tel: 01 43 375 100
HOURS 9 A.M. TO MIDNIGHT

24-HOUR OPTICIAN
SOS Optique
Tel: 01 48 072 200
www.sosoptique.com
They offer 24-hour repair for
glasses and even deliver. The
web site includes a small section
in English.

24-HOUR PHARMACY
All pharmacies in France bear
a green neon cross that serves
as an indicator of their services.
It's as universal as McDonald's
golden arches. Pharmacists in
France are highly skilled and can
provide basic medical advice as
well as serve as a mini-medical
clinic for such minor needs as
disinfecting and bandaging
small cuts and bruises.
> Pharmacie Européenne
6 place de Clichy, 9ᵉ
Tel: 01 48 746 518
> Derhy/Pharmacie des Champs-Elysées
84, av des Champs-Elysées, 8ᵉ
Tel: 01 45 620 241
> Pharma Presto
Tel 01 61 040 404
www.pharma-presto.com
These folks will deliver and have
been known to chauffeur pets
to the vet. The delivery charge
is €40 from 8 a.m. to 6 p.m. and
€55 from 6 p.m. to 8 a.m. and on
weekends.

24-HOUR POST OFFICE
The Poste Centrale du Louvre is
open 24 hours a day, seven days a
week. Stamps for postcards
can also be bought from any *tabac*
(cigarette and sundries) shop.
> Poste Centrale du Louvre
52, rue du Louvre, 2ᵉ
Tel: 01 40 282 000

GETTING AROUND IN THE CITY OF LIGHT
Métro, Buses and Taxi
To find street signs in Paris, look
up. They are attached to the first
and last buildings of the street.
At one time, it was compulsory
for the owners of the first and
the last house of each street to
engrave the street name. Note
that the *arrondissements* (1-20)
are usually included in the street
signs as well. This is indicated
by the last two digits of the zip
code. The initial '75' stands for
Paris, so 75007 means you are in
the 7ᵉ arrondissement of Paris.
Simple, *non*?

The subway in Paris is called the
métro. It generally runs from
about 6 a.m. to 1 a.m. and is the
most economical and fastest way
to get around the city, other than
by bicycle. The *métro* is generally
safe, but as with every major
metropolitan hub, you should
always be on the lookout for
pickpockets and other hazards.
Be sure to hold on to your ticket
for random checks, you'll get a

hefty fine if you don't have one. You will also need your ticket to exit from a métro station. A helpful web site is: www.ratp.info. Children under the age of 10 are eligible for discounted tickets, called *billet demi-tarif* (half-priced tickets).

However, Paris is truly not a stroller-friendly city, and lugging a buggy up and down the *métro* stairs isn't much fun. In addition to the mostly small and narrow pedestrian sidewalks above ground, the turnstiles and millions of stairs found in most *métro* stations can be difficult and stressful to navigate. Consider taking the **bus**, when you can. Turn necessity into a virtue by selling this to your kids as a sightseeing tour. Many of the buses have priority seats in the front for parents traveling with kids under four years old. This lucky group of under-four jet-setters also travels on the bus for free, while their older siblings, from four to 10 years old, travel for half price.

A couple of things to note about traveling by bus: First of all, you need to purchase another ticket for transfers. You can buy your bus ticket when you get on the bus, and correct change is appreciated. On buses, all tickets need to be punched into a machine that is located next to the driver. The standard fare is €1.40. Single-journey tickets can be bought on the bus. If you think you'll be riding the métro or bus several times, get the most bang for your buck by purchasing a 10-ticket *carnet* for €10.50. Tickets can be bought at most *tabacs* (cigarette shops), *métro* stations, and tourist offices.

A few things to consider about traffic in Paris: pedestrians, *en garde!* Traffic in Paris is increasing each day, like in any big city. Cars, trucks, mopeds, and motorcycles drive fast and try to make the next light—no matter what. There's a campaign to educate drivers to show more consideration and awareness for bikes, pedestrians, etc., but don't be surprised if you see cars racing through yellow and even red lights. Also be aware of *priorité de droite* (priority on the right). This means that whoever is approaching an intersection from the right side has the right of way; otherwise you must yield. Merging into traffic, need to make a turn? Look right *and* left, but always to the right. Pedestrians and bicyclists stay alert: it is only valid if you are driving a motorized vehicle. Also, since motorists are mostly concerned about other cars coming from the right, they won't always look left: a real danger for you when you are trying to cross the street, even at a marked crosswalk.

Every official **taxi** has a light on the roof that indicates whether it's in service, already has a passenger, or is available for passenger pick-ups. If a taxi has a white light on, it's available. An orange light indicates the cab is already taken. Generally speaking, it's hard to find a taxi during rush hour and in the early part of the morning. There are many *station de taxis* (taxi stands) located at major intersections, at bus and *métro* stations, where you can hail a taxi. These taxi stands are marked with a blue sign.

Be advised: if you call for a taxi or even hail one from down the street, the meter starts ticking from the moment they start the engine. Taxis normally take a maximum of three passengers. They may charge for a fourth person, and there is a €2 fee for a stroller.

> *Taxis Bleus*
Tel: 01 49 361 010
www.taxis-bleus.com

> *G7*
Tel: 01 47 394 739
Tel in English: 01 41 276 699
www.taxis-g7.fr

An alternative option is to take the **Batobus**, a water taxi that travels up and down the Seine. It hits all the "must-see" hotspots, including the Eiffel Tower, *Musée du Louvre*, *Musée d'Orsay* and *Notre-Dame* Cathedral, to name a few. Purchase a day pass and you can get on and off as often as you like. There are a total of eight sightseeing stops. For more information and further timetables, see the **Beauty and the Beast** section, under *Bateaux Parisiens*.

LOST PROPERTY
Bureau des Objets Trouvés
36 rue des Morillons, 15ᵉ
Métro: Convention
Tel: 01 55 762 000
Tel in English: 08 21 002 525
Hours: mon to thu 8 a.m. to 5 p.m.; fri 8:30 a.m. to 4:30 p.m.
Tues/Thurs: 8:30 a.m. to 8 p.m.
This place has been located at the same address since 1804. Valuable objects are kept for three years. Every year, the department handles about 30,000 items, yet only hundreds are reunited with their owners. That's probably due to the fact that most items are only kept three months. You will need to visit in person to fill out a lost property form.

LOST OR STOLEN CREDIT CARDS
Visa: 08 92 70 57 05
Visa Premier: 08 92 70 57 05
American Express: 01 47 77 70 00
Eurocard : 01 45 67 84 84
Diner's Club: 08 10 31 41 59

HOTELS AND PLACES TO STAY
Contact the Paris Convention and Visitors Bureau at www.paris-touristoffice.com to obtain a list of

the city's 2,000 hotels. In France, all hotels charge an additional room tax, known as *taxe de séjour*. The tax rate is about €1 per person. Most hotels are fully booked during the major trade fairs in January, May and September. Also keep in mind the Fashion weeks, which take place in January, March, early July and October. During the low season – July and August – hotels often offer special deals and discounts.

EATING OUT

Most Parisians have lunch from 1 p.m. to 2 p.m. Dinner usually starts around 8 p.m. or 8:30 p.m. for adults. However restaurants start serving dinner at 7 p.m. Restaurants in Paris tend to offer children mini-portions of what a self-respecting adult would eat. Just about every cafe offers the traditional *croque monsieur*—like a grilled cheese with thin slices of ham on toast. There is always the reliable *steak-frites*—not a fried steak, but a steak served with French fries. Besides McDonald's—and there seem to be hundreds of them in central Paris—another chain to keep in mind is the Hippopotamus restaurants. It's the Parisian equivalent of Chuck 'E' Cheese without the play areas. The Hippopotamus chain is a good, reliable and relatively healthy place to eat with children. It's on a higher nutrition level than fast food,

and it's as family-friendly as you can get, offering fast service, a children's menu and a coloring book with crayons. Most of the Hippopotamus restaurants in Paris also provide a child activity fun packet, guaranteed to keep the kids entertained. Another family friendly restaurant chain is *Léon de Bruxelles*. There are several in the Paris. (See **Eats** listing for both *Hippopotamus* and *Léon de Bruxelles*.)

Bistros: Bistros are the French equivalent of American diners or English pubs. The word bistro stems from the Russian word bystro, which literally translates as 'hurry'. Russian soldiers occupying France after the Napoleonic Wars would demand that their food be served quickly, by shouting the word that then evolved into the term "bistro". There is a bistro located on practically every street corner in Paris. Here you can find your *lentilles, soupe à l'oignon, bœuf bourguignon, coq au vin* and *mousse au chocolat* (otherwise known as lentils, onion soup, beef stewed in red wine, chicken stewed in white wine, and chocolate pudding— but doesn't it sound so much better in French). And don't forget to wash it all down with a good, cheap bottle of wine. For kids, you'll find that *croque monsieur* or *croque madame* (grilled cheese, ham and fried egg), and you'll be hard pressed *not* to find steak-frites.

With kids, it's best to make reservations and/or go rather early, keeping in mind that most restaurants don't start serving dinner until 7 p.m. to 7:30 p.m. By going early, chances are you can be seated in just about any restaurant in town—without having to wait. This also works at home: if you see a kid's menu offered, it's a good indicator that children are welcome.

Lunch options: Find a pleasant-looking sandwich shop. You are, after all, in the land of baguettes and fizzy water. Then, head to one of the many parks in Paris and have an impromptu *pique-nique*: another term the French invented. Alternatively, make lunch your main meal of the day. It can be easier to get a table in the restaurants, the food is often cheaper (even for the same meal), and the kids aren't as tired and whiny (nor are the other patrons). Plus, with a light dinner in the evening, you can get to bed earlier and wake well rested and ready for a new day. If you are a coffee drinker and on a budget, it's cheaper to order your coffee at the bar of the café and drink it standing. But if you're with children, you will probably want a table. A few Parisian etiquette tips for dining out: be sure to say *bon jour* (hello) when entering any establishment and *merci* (thank you) when you leave (this goes for shops as well as eateries). This is customary Parisian etiquette, and it's considered bad manners not to do so. Also, be sure to address adult men as *Monsieur* meaning "sir"; use *Madame* when you would use "Mrs." in English and *Mademoiselle* when speaking to an unmarried woman. If you aren't sure about the woman, stick with *Madame*. Finally, regardless of what you might have learned in your high school French class, if you need assistance in a restaurant, DO NOT shout *"garçon,"* which literally translates as 'boy". The correct term to use is: *"s'il vous plaît,"* or if you please.

TIPPING

A 15% service charge is always added to every restaurant bill in France. It's the law, no matter what type of service you receive, good or bad. You will see it noted on the bill as *service compris*. This tax leaves the customer under no obligation to tip further. While many Parisians won't tip, if you feel your service was particularly noteworthy, by all means leave a little extra cash with your bill. One possibility is to round up to the nearest euro. You can also consider leaving around €5 to €10 for a restaurant bill of €100. It is customary to tip 10% for taxis.

PLANNING YOUR VISIT: FRENCH SCHOOL HOLIDAY CALENDAR

When planning around the school holiday calendar, don't forget about weekends and Wednesday afternoons. On Wednesdays throughout France, most children attend school for only part of the day so be prepared for longish lines as most child-friendly destinations in Paris will be full of (surprise, surprise) kids. Other periods to keep in mind: a two-week school holiday in mid-February; Easter (late March, early April); a school holiday at the end of October/beginning of November; and summer break all of July and August. Many attractions are closed when schools are closed (if it's a national holiday), so be sure to plan ahead. On the other hand, others add extra hours on Wednesdays and during the summer. One of the best sources for fact checking addresses, timings and holiday schedules is the French Tourist Office web site: www.francetourism.com. Another site to try is the National Education web site at www.education.gouv.fr

CALENDAR OF CAN'T MISS, FAMILY-FRIENDLY EVENTS

January: For those born to shop, this is definitely a great time to be in Paris. During the winter sales *(soldes)*, huge discounts of up to 75% can be found for the true bargain hunters. Low season also means great deals on flights to the City of Light.

February: Chinese New Year. A delightful parade in a sea of red and gold—the traditional Chinese good luck colors—down Paris's famed Avenue des Champs-Elysées. There are giant floats, dancing dragons, and thousands of costumed performers, acrobats, and musicians. Even the Eiffel Tower gets in on the act: it's bathed in a red light, in honor of the Chinese New Year.

Late May, early June: French Open. It is one of the biggest sporting events in France and the second of the Grand Slam tournaments. This event is held every year at the famous Roland-Garros Tennis Center.

Mid-June: *Déjeuner sur l'Herbe* (Lunch on the Lawn). An elegant outdoor fête held at the chateau of *Vaux-le-Vicomte*, with more than 2,000 visitors wearing 17th and 18th-century costumes, singing and dancing all day and into the night.

June 21st: *Fête de la Musique* (Music Festival). Cellists have been known to descend on the Seine on rafts; marching bands gather together and toot their horns on the steps of the *Académie Française*, and romantic music lovers fill concert venues at the

Eiffel Tower, *Place de la Bastille* and the *Place de la Concorde*. Parisians of all ages flood the streets, block traffic, dance, laugh, sing and dine while listening to musicians from all over the world performing free concerts all night long. It's the world's biggest block party.

July 14th: Bastille Day Don't think that the U.S. is the only country celebrating a colorful past with fireworks in July. The fun actually starts here on the evening of July 13th, with les bals des pompiers—parties held at the fire stations. The 14th marks the start of the French Revolution that toppled King Louis XVI and the aristocracy.

July: *Le Tour de France* Held each year, this is the world's largest and most famous cycling event. Riders cover 2000 miles in just 21 days. Millions of people flock to the *Avenue des Champs-Elysées* to embrace the winner. There is plenty of champagne, wine and crêpes on hand. For more information, visit the official web site at www.letour.fr

Mid-July to Mid-August: *Paris Plage* (Paris Beach). Now in its sixth consecutive year, *Paris Plage* is a manmade beach along the River Seine that turns the river banks into a two-mile beach party. This summer hot spot is furnished with palm trees, loungers, hammocks, trampolines and tons—20,000 tons to be exact—of sand. The site offers several small cafes and showers, too. It's a seaside paradise in the city for kids.

July 15th to the end of August: *Festival du Cinema en Plein Air* (Open-air Cinema Festival). This event is held in the *Parc de la Villette* every evening except Monday. People head to the park with picnic baskets and *pâté* to watch free movies outdoors. Home to Europe's largest inflatable screen, the films range from cinema classics to new releases.

September: It's not the London Eye, but you can get a bird's eye view of Paris from Place de la Concorde's **Grande Roue** (ferris wheel) starting this month until March.
MÉTRO: CONCORDE (LINE 1, 8, 12)
HOURS: 10:30 A.M. TO MIDNIGHT
COST: €8

Second weekend of September: *Fêtes des Jardins de Paris* (Festival of Parisian Gardens). Hundreds of free exhibitions and gardens dolled up for the occasion. Take a new and unique look at the city's green spaces.

Last weekend in September: *Journées du Patrimoine* (Heritage Days). Open house for just about every historic monument and site across France.

First weekend in October: *Fête des Vendanges* (Wine Harvest Festival) in *Montmartre*. Yes, there are wine-producing vineyards in Paris—right on the *butte* of *Montmartre*. Every year since 1935, Parisians have been celebrating this fact with a weekend harvest party.

Mid-October until late February: *Cirque d'Hiver Bouglione* (Bouglione Winter Circus). As traditional as it gets in the world of circus entertainment, the Bouglione circus has been around for several generations—close to seven decades. Housed in one of the most beautiful 19th-century venues Paris has to offer.

December: Tis' the season to be merry and a bevy of merry-go-rounds pop up all over Paris to mark the occasion The **Manèges de Noël** can be found in squares around Paris including *Hôtel de Ville, Place Saint-Sulpice* and the *Square du Temple.*
MÉTRO: HÔTEL DE VILLE (LINE 1); SAINT-SULPICE (LINE 4); SQUARE DU TEMPLE (LINE 1)
HOURS: 10:30 A.M. TO 7:30 P.M. DAILY.
COS: FREE

Ice-skating: Every winter, a large ice-rink is created outside the Hôtel de Ville which is a hit with locals and tourists. It's an annual event and the rink is active from December to March.
Métro: Hôtel de Ville or Châtelet (line 1, 4, 11)

Hours: Open Mon-Thu 12 P.M. TO 10 P.M.; Fri 12 P.M. TO Midnight; Sat 9 A.M. TO Midnight; Sun 9 A.M. TO 10 P.M.
Cost: There is no cost to use the rink, but skate hire is €5.

>*Patinoire Montparnasse* also attracts crowds with its ice-skating ring.
MÉTRO: MONTPARNASSE (LINE 4)
HOURS: MON TO FRI 12 P.M. TO 8 P.M.; SAT AND SUN 9 A.M. TO 8 P.M.
COST: FREE, BUT SKATE HIRE IS €5

Christmas markets: Celebrate the season with several Christmas markets around the city. You can find decorations, gifts, vin chaud (hot wine) and an abundance of tasty treats. Here are a few worth visiting:
> *La Défense* under the Grand Arch *Parvis de la Défense*
MÉTRO: LA DEFENSE
TIMINGS: LATE NOV 29 TO DEC 29
OFFERINGS: LOTS OF FOOD AND LOTS OF KITSCH
> **Santa's Village,** Latin Quarter Boulevard Saint-Germain
MÉTRO: SAINT-GERMAIN OR SAINT-MICHEL
TIMINGS: FIRST WEEK IN DEC TO NEW YEAR'S EVE
> **Christmas market** at *Saint-Sulpice*, Place Saint-Sulpice, 6e
MÉTRO: SAINT-SULPICE
TIMINGS: FIRST WEEK OF DEC TO CHRISTMAS EVE
> *Les Féeries d'Auteuil*
40 eue Jean de la Fontaine, 16e
METRO: JASMIN, EGLISE D'AUTEUIL
BUS: 22, 52, 62,70, 72 (MAISON DE LA RADIO)
TIMINGS: DEC. 1 TO CHRISTMAS EVE
OFFERINGS: CRECHE, CONCERTS, GIFTS AND FOOD

>Maison de l'Alsace
39 avenue des Champs-Elysées, 8e
Métro: Champs- Elysées
Timings: Dec. 1 to Dec. 28

Spring, summer and autumn:
Funfairs: There are several
throughout the season, with the
best being **La Fête a Neu-Neu** in
the *Bois de Boulogne* (autumn); the
Foire du Trône in *Bois de Vincennes*
(spring); and **La Fête des Tuileries**
in the *Jardin des Tuileries* (summer)
with a landmark ferris wheel,
making this a triple-tie for the fun
fair best-of-show.

A FEW WORDS ON MUSEUM VISITS

Your best bet is the **Carte
Musées et Monuments** (Museum
and Monument Pass), which
will save money and time. It
covers nearly 70 participating
museums and monuments. For
a complete list of attractions
and point-of-sale venues where
you can purchase the pass, see
www.parismuseumpass.fr or
www.intermusees.com
Although children under 18
have free admission to most
museums and monuments, this
card will allow parents to skip the
ticket line—a big plus with so
many places to see and so little
time, especially when traveling
en famille. There are one-day
(€15), three-day (€30), and five
day (€45) passes available. Be
advised: passes must be used on
consecutive days, and you get
unlimited admission. Best of all,
you only need to visit two sights
a day to break even!

There are also several well-known
museums open until late in the
evening, and some of these are less
crowded at night. At last count,
there were more than 130 museums
in Paris, but here are a few child-
friendly options with night visits:
Musée Picasso, open Thursdays until 8 p.m.
Musée du Louvre, open Wednesdays
until 9:45 p.m.;
Musée d'Orsay, open Thursdays
until 9:45 p.m.;
**Centre National d'Art et de Culture
Georges Pompidou,** open until 9 p.m.

Most museums offer free
admission one day a month. Also,
most state-run museums in France
close one day a week, generally on
either Monday or Tuesday. Hours
are usually fixed, but be sure to
double check opening and closing
times with your hotel before you
plan your itinerary each day.
Family hint: To keep kids
entertained while you soak in the
culture, try visiting the museum
shop before beginning your visit. Let
each kid pick a postcard of an item
they like in the museum collection,
and make a treasure hunt of
finding this picture, sculpture, etc.
Just make sure the item is actually
on display in the museum—the
shops often sell postcards of things
in other collections.

CONVERSION CHART FOR CHILDREN'S CLOTHING

Clothes (in inches)											
Age	3 m	6 m	12 m	18 m	2 y	3 y	4 y	6 y	8 y	10 y	12 y	14 y
Stature	24	26.8	29.6	32.4	34.4	37.6	40.8	45.6	50.4	55.2	60	62.4
Waist measur.	16	17.6	18.4	19.2	19.6	20	20.8	21.6	22.4	23.2	24	24.8
Hip measur.	15.2	17.2	19.2	21.2	22.4	23	23.6	26.4	28	30.4	33.6	35.6
Head circum.	17.2	18	18.8	20	20.4	20.8	21.2	21.6	22	22.4	22.8	22.8

Shoes															
French Foot size	18	19	20	21	22	23	23.5	24	25	26	26.5	27	27.5	28	29	29.5
UK size	2	3	4	5	5.5	6	6.5	7	7.5	8	8.5	9	9.5	10	10.5	11
US size	3.5	4.5	5.5	6.5	7	7.5	8	8.5	9	9.5	10	10.5	11	11.5	12	12.5
Centimeters	12	12.7	13.3	14	14.7	15.3	15.7	16	16.7	17.3	17.6	18	18.3	18.6	19.3	19.6
Inches	4.72	4.98	5.24	5.51	5.77	6.03	6.16	6.29	6.56	6.82	6.95	7.08	7.21	7.34	7.60	7.74
French Foot size	30	31	31.5	32	33	33.5	34	35	35.5	36	37	37.5	38	38.5	39	
UK size	11.5	12	12.5	13	13.5	1	1.5	2	2.5	3	3.5	4	4.5	5	5.5	
US size	13	13.5	1	1.5	2	2.5	3	3.5	4	4.5	5	5.5	6	6.5	7	
Centimeters	20	20.6	21	21.3	22	22.3	22.6	23.3	23.6	24	24.6	25	25.3	25.6	26	
Inches	7.87	8.13	8.26	8.39	8.65	8.78	8.91	9.18	9.31	9.44	9.7	9.83	9.96	10.09	10.23	

CURRENCY

The monetary unit is the euro. There are currency exchange places all over Paris as well as an abundance of ATMs. If you would rather do your transactions at a bank, hours are 9 a.m. to 4:30 p.m. Mon to Fri.

STORE HOURS

Generally, stores open from 10 a.m. to 7 p.m. There are a few major department stores which open late one evening each week until 9:30 or 10 p.m. Beware of the traditional Parisian lunch hour (1 p.m.-2 p.m.) when planning any shopping. You are better off doing as the Parisians do, and grabbing some lunch instead. Don't count on stores to be open on Sundays, except for *boulangeries* and *patisseries* (bakeries and pastry shops), which are open on Sunday mornings. Sundays are the day for outdoor markets (farmers' markets, flea markets, etc.) and almost all shops are closed. Although it may seem as if the city is sleeping all day, a few shops open on the *Avenue des Champs-Elysées*, in particular: the Disney store, the Virgin Megastore and the Publicis Drugstore, which offers everything from bandages and newspapers to designer clothing and *baguettes* and *brie*, and pretty much everything in between.

A word on the twice-yearly seasonal *les soldes* (sales): everyone is an educated consumer in France, especially since the seasonal sales are strictly regulated by law. There is an official opening day and any attempt to cheat is severely punished by a hefty fine. A special brigade controls that the discounted goods are actual inventory clearance, and not just cheaper stuff that was brought in the shop just before the sale period. Even the word *"soldes"* cannot be used outside the official sales periods.

Be sure if you're from outside the European Union to also inquire about your 12% tax refund for any purchase over €175 bought the same day in the same store. The paper transaction for the tax refund occurs within minutes after your purchase. Just remember to ask for it.

A NOTE ABOUT TOILETS

If you have a youngster who needs to "go," take advantage of the adequate facilities available in restaurants and public places (sometimes for a small fee). Generally, at Hippopotamus, *Léon de Bruxelles*, and other family-oriented restaurants, the facilities are clean and basic. There is also a MacDonald's in nearly every neighborhood that you can duck into. Most museums have reasonable facilities. Most of these facilities will not offer a changing table and may be up or down a (sometimes steep) set of stairs. The street toilets may not be the most glamorous "monuments" you visit when you are in Paris,

but they are undoubtedly some of the most useful. There are 420 of these public toilets in Paris and they are now completely free of charge (until recently you had to pay about 20 cents). The big advantage is that they are automatically cleaned every time someone uses them. It's a big step up compared to the previous model (*les vespasiennes*, named after Roman Emperor Vespasian) of which only one example is still in use (in the Luxembourg gardens, if you are really curious).

Parents' tip: Browse www.thebathroomdiaries.com/france/paris to get locations of toilets around the city and a rating on the cleanliness. Bookmark this site for future globetrotting. Do remember to pack a folding potty seat cover. Onestepahead sells one for $12.95 which comes with handles, so the kiddies don't have to touch the toilet in their effort to balance. Have a pack of wet wipes handy to clean the bottom of the seat before folding it away. Another option is disposable toilet seat covers that come in a 10-pack for $6.95.

ADAPTERS

Electricity in France runs on a 220-volt current. Most U.S. appliances operate on 110 volts. Therefore, you will need a voltage converter to charge the DVD player, game boy and cell phone (if it's GSM enabled or it will be rendered useless). Many travel stores in airports and elsewhere (Brookstone) throughout the U.S. will offer lightweight and pocket-sized converters and plugs. In Paris, try the shop *B.H.V.*

> **Bazar de l'Hôtel de Ville**
52-64 rue de Rivoli, 1ᵉ
TEL: 01 42 749 000

SWIMMING

Most public pools in Paris and the rest of France require swimming caps for every one and ban Bermuda-style swimming trunks for men and boys. Generally, upscale hotels tend to be more flexible with foreign visitors regarding the dress code.

A MUST-READ

Pick up the weekly publication *Pariscope* (in French) for additional child-friendly information on circuses, marionette shows, special events and other entertainment. The English-language *Paris Voice* is an additional, comprehensive source. Both publications can be purchased from most newsstands.

OFF WE GO!

Where to begin? Paris is a walking city—in fact, it is possible to cross the city on foot in about three hours—so what you put on your feet is important. If you have a pair of stilettos that are comfortable on grates and cobblestone, go for it. Otherwise, a better bet is a fashionable pair of sneakers or sandals. Try the hip and moderately priced *Campers* brand from Spain. With many boutiques in Paris, this brand offers flat-heeled and fashionable footwear; see **Shopping** for addresses. There are more than 20 cities in the U.S. that sell Campers, or they can be ordered on the Web at http://www.camper.com. A good map of Paris is the next travel essential needed to begin exploring Paris and its 20 arrondissements (neighborhoods) spiraling out from Point Zero in front of *Notre-Dame* Cathedral. The Seine River divides the city (and some say the ambiance) between the *Rive Droite* (Right Bank) to the north of the river and the *Rive Gauche* (Left Bank) to the south.

Tour Eiffel—the Eiffel Tower—is the city's top destination for children of all ages. It's a good idea to make this the first place to visit as it offers pure visual pleasure at its best for the out-of-town guest. Mom's hint: hike up to the 2ⁿᵈ-floor landing with the kids, and then take the elevator to the top. The lines are much shorter on the 2nd floor, and the kids get a bit of exercise and will hit the sack hard at day's end so you can enjoy a nice glass of wine. (For more information, check out **If you have to be a tourist**).

Back on the ground, with legs feeling like they are about to fall off, stay in the neighborhood and hop aboard one of the *bateaux mouches,* the tourist boats that cruise the Seine. You can't miss the boat connection—it is literally at the base of the Eiffel Tower. The *bateaux mouches* are to Paris what gondolas are to Venice. However, you may want to push the visit to the Eiffel Tower and the boat ride until dusk as both are also excellent choices for an evening visit. The lights from passing boats on the Seine provide a magic lantern show, and the skyline views from the top of the Eiffel Tower will clearly show you the real answer to why Paris is the world's most romantic city. For extra sparkle, make sure to catch a view of the Eiffel Tower after sundown: each hour from sundown to 2 a.m., the lights fizzle like a glass of champagne for 10 minutes. (This special-effects feature was created for the millennium celebrations in 2000.)

> Eiffel Tower Champ-de-Mars
Métro: Bir-Hakeim, Trocadero, Ecole Militaire Bus: 42, 69, 72, 82, 87
Tel: 33 (0) 1 44 11 23 23

Hours: Every day all year long, 9:30 a.m. to 11p.m., Jan 1 to June 14 and Sept 2 to Dec 31; from 9 a.m. to midnight, June 15 to Sept 1.
Tickets: Prices range from €2.30 to €11.50 depending on whether you take the elevator, stairs, stop at one level or go all the way to the top.
www.tour-eiffel.fr/teiffel/uk

> Bateaux Mouches Base of the Eiffel Tower
Hours: 10 a.m. to 11 p.m., departs every 30 min
Apr to Sept; 11 a.m. to 9 p.m., departs every 45 min Oct to March
Tickets: Adults €8, €4 ages 4 to 12; free for children under 4
www.bateaux-mouches.fr

Les Colonnes Morris

(The Morris Columns)
Look up! It's not a bird, it's not a plane, it's ... *Les Colonnes Morris* (Morris Columns), and they are all over Paris—and very typically Parisian. At last count, there were about 790 of these columns in the streets of Paris. They are used to promote cultural events such as plays, concerts and exhibitions, and some are used as public toilets (inside, of course). There are even a few which include public phones (mostly on the Champs-Elysées). They are called the Morris Columns after their inventor, Gabriel Morris.

BEAUTY AND THE BEAST

Keep your little angels and mini-monsters
entertained with fabulous outdoor fun in the city.
Jardin du Luxembourg (Luxembourg Garden),
*Marionettes du Luxembourg, Bois de Vincennes
- Parc Zoologique de Paris* (the Paris Zoo) and *Parc
Floral de Paris* (the Paris Flower Park), *Ferme de
Paris* (the Paris Farm) and *Buteaux Parisiens* –
the best tourist boat operator on the Seine.
Also don't let the *"Pelouse Interdite"* (Keep off
the Grass) signs scare you and your offspring.
Paris may seem daunting for the parent traveling
with young people, but its many green spaces,
with and without the fortified grass humans are
allowed on, keep both local and touring parents
sane. Keep in mind that many of the parks include
both free playgrounds, and playgrounds you must
pay to enter.

Jardin du Luxembourg

(Luxembourg Garden). Firmly planted in the *6e arrondissement*, and bordered by the 5e and 14e, the Luxembourg Garden is one of the most popular city parks in Paris. This is probably because there is a grassy area you can actually walk and run on. General rule in Paris: you must be accompanied by a toddler to enjoy this luxury. Plus, with its 56 acres of formal gardens, child-friendly lawns, playgrounds, puppet theatre, carousel, old-fashioned swings, sandboxes, wading pools, toy sailboats, *Grand Bassin* (a lake with ducks and fish), gazebo, beehives, pétanque, ponies, and cafés—well, you get the idea—a kid can be happily distracted for hours here. There are even pedal-powered cars available near the park's southern edge.

> ### Jardin du Luxer~~~
boulevard Saint~~
MÉTRO: ODÉON
TEL: 01 42 342 023
HOURS: DAILY
COST: FREE (RIDES COST EXTRA)

There are both free and pay playgrounds and sandpits. The old-fashioned carousel and swings charge a nominal fee, and your child will probably ask for the *barbe à papa* (cotton candy) sold at the snack booth, so be ready with money in hand. Be sure to get your hands stamped at any of the pay playgrounds. This will enable you to re-enter the playground without paying twice. Children can also ride Shetland ponies for a small charge.

Parent's hint: Install your older children in the fenced-in, pay playground while you sip a *café viennois* or a beer, depending on your preference (and perhaps the hour), at the café just outside.

Sailboats: These can be rented on Wednesdays, weekends and school holidays. The sailboats are not battery-operated; they are actually toy schooners that sail across the ponds with just the push of a stick. The same sailboats can be found in the ***Jardin des Tuileries*** (Tuileries Gardens), known for its spectacularly enormous bronze statues.

Merry-go-round: One of most beloved merry-go-rounds in Paris is located here. The adorable wooden animals are a treasure trove you won't want to miss. They were designed by the world-famous 19th-century architect, Charles Garnier—who also designed the Paris Opera house.

Jardin des Tuileries, Bordering Place de la Concorde
MÉTRO: TUILERIES OR CONCORDE
TEL: 01 40 209 043
HOURS: DAILY 7:30 A.M. TO 7 P.M.
COST: FREE

Next to the merry-go-round is another top choice: the best marionette theater in Paris, **Marionettes du Luxembourg.** Since 1933 the Desarthis family has owned and operated the puppet theater. The 40 minute show changes periodically but always showcases the world-renowned *Guignol*. This famous French puppet hero has been around since the 18th century. You can't miss him: children go ga-ga over him as soon as he appears on stage. Traditionally, French children scream his name in unison as soon as he appears on stage. To get into the fun, try pronouncing it "Gee-niol" (with a hard "G"). *Guignol* always enlists the help of the audience, as he tries to catch villains, get out of trouble or request some simple advice. The shows are performed entirely in French, but don't worry: children will have no problem understanding the plots to the well-known fairytales in bedtime stories .Theater staff members ring a cow bell outside the theater before each show, to let people know it's time to line up for the performance. A nice stroller parking area is provided.

Marionettes du Luxem ͨ

Jardin du Luxemℒ
boulevard Saint-Michℒ
Métro: Odéon, Notre-Dame
des Champs
RER Luxembourg
Park entrances: rue de Medicis,
rue Guynemer, blvd. St-Michel,
rue de Vaugirard.
Tel: 01 43 264 647
Hours: Performances are held Wed
at 4 p.m. and Sat and Sun at 11 a.m.
and 4 p.m.
Cost: €3.50 per person, including
children.

GUIGNOL

Other puppet shows
Marionnettes du Champ-de-Mars, Champ-de-Mars
Métro: Ecole Militaire
Tel: 01 48 560 144
Hours: Wed, Sat and Sun, 3:15 p.m. to 4:15 p.m.
Cost: €2.50

Marionnettes des Champs-Elysées
Rond point des Champs-Elysées
Métro: Champs-Elysées -Clémenceau
01 40 354 720
Hours: Wed, Sat and Sun; 3 p.m. 4 p.m. and 5 p.m.
Cost: €2.90

FYI: Did you know that there are not one, but two Statues of Liberty in Paris? The most famous is located on the *Allée des Cygnes* (Swan Island), while the other one is located in the Luxembourg Garden (on the rue Guynemer side). It served as a model for sculptor Frédéric Bartholdi before he made the "real one," which was given to the Americans in 1885.
> Statue of Liberty,
Allée des Cygnes
Métro: Javel

Another tidbit: be sure to investigate the beehives. There are about 10 of them and they are used to train future apiculturists to harvest honey, which is then sold each year in the nearby *Orangerie*. These beehives are protected by a fence so that children and their parents can't get too close to the bees.

Gotta go? A note on toilets: Inside the fee-paying playground, there are two adult restrooms and one kids-only restroom with all the fixtures in miniature. A padded changing table is available. There are also toilets below the café near the reflecting pool and near the basketball court. These charge a small fee and are accessible via stairs.

Bois de Vincennes (Vincennes Park): The *Bois de Vincennes* offers more than 500 acres of activities for children of all ages and their families. It is the largest park in Paris, accessible by *métro* just east of the city limits. It is also home to two other child-friendly attractions: the ***Parc Zoologique de Paris***

(the Paris Zoo) and **Parc Floral de Paris** (the Paris Flower Park). Within the park there are three lakes: *Lac de Saint Mande, Lac Minimes* and *Lac Daumesnil*. There is an array of fun for children, including paddleboats, bicycling (see below for rental information), rollerblading, skateboarding, etc. There is also a working farm on the premises called **Ferme de Paris** (the Paris Farm) where children can feed barnyard animals such as chickens, goats, and lambs. The *Parc Zoologique de Paris* is located in the heart of the *Bois de Vincennes*—you can't miss it, just look for the *Grand Rocher*, the 236 foot-tall artificial mountain, and go for it. The main zoo in Paris, it is also one of the largest in Europe. For over 50 years, the permanent collection has housed more than 600 species in what seems to be almost their natural habitats. From baboons to lemurs to giant pandas, they are all here. Be sure to read the notice board at the entrance for listings of any newborns and to check the feeding schedule. Big hits with little folk: feeding times for the pandas, seals and sea lions. And, above all, don't miss the miniature steam train that runs around the zoo's perimeter, allowing little ones to get a peek of what's in store for them inside. Be advised that the zoo tends to get crowded on weekends. While in the Bois de Vincennes,

be sure to visit *Parc Floral de Paris*, another one of the city's best play areas for children. There is a miniature train, nature center, butterfly garden and an amazing playground. Older children will also enjoy the mini-golf or the race track with pedal-powered horses. On Wednesday afternoons, there are free theater shows.

> **Parc Zoologique de Paris,**
53 av de St. Maurice,
Bois de Vincennes, 12e.
MÉTRO: PORTE DORÉE
BUS: 46, 325, PARC ZOOLOGIQUE 86
TEL: 01 44 752 000
HOURS: 9 A.M. TO 5 P.M.
www.parcfloraldeparis.com
For more information on playgrounds and the Jardin d'Acclimatation (Zoological Gardens), see the *Boat crew* Paradise section.

Bateaux Parisiens: For a really atmospheric experience, take a ride day or night on a *bateau mouche,* the tourist boats that cruise up and down the River Seine. Kids love to go under the bridges. The best operator for children is the *Bateaux Parisiens*. These folks offer a variety of boat trips—some including entertainment for kids, others with food (the dinner cruise/night tour is delightful; probably best for you and your older children). During school holidays and weekends, they offer a special *Croisière Enchantée* (Enchanted

Jardin d'Acclimatation

Cruise) for children aged 3 to 10 years old. The ride includes elves that sing songs and tell stories about the monuments you will be sailing past. (In French, but with lots of miming.) There's an early-evening option and headphones are available in 13 languages.

Be on the lookout for the miniature Statue of Liberty by sculptor Frederic Bartholdi. This bronze replica of the Statue of Liberty (it's "only" 35 feet high) was a gift from the American community in Paris on July 4, 1889. By the way, the engineer who designed the interior structure, Gustave Eiffel, is—you guessed it—the same fellow who designed the Eiffel Tower.
Parent's hint: If traveling with young children, try to schedule your boat trip in the early part

of the day. Little ones have been known to fall asleep on this one-hour boat ride—kind of like when you used to rock your children to sleep.

> *Bateaux Parisiens,* At the foot of the Eiffel Tower
Métro: Bir-Hakeim-Grenelle.
Tel: 01 46 994 313
Hours: Every 30 min from 10 a.m. to 11 p.m. Apr to Sept (high season); every hour with a few half-hourly departures from 10 a.m. to 11 p.m. Oct to March (low season). No departure at 1:30 p.m.
www.bateauxparisiens.com
Details for *Croisière Enchantée:*
October to June, including Wednesdays. Summer special from July 1 to 12 at 3 p.m. Closed from July 13 to the end of Sept.
Tickets: €9.50 per person. Children pay the same fare.

DIVAS

The hot spots for girls out on the town. Turn
favorite pastimes into a cultural event, and more.
Musée de la Poupée (Doll Museum), *Opéra Garnier*,
Musée d'Eventail (Fan Museum), *Musée de la
Mode et du Costume* (Museum of Fashion),
Fashion shows at *Printemps* and *Galeries
Lafayette*, Cooking Schools, *Marché aux Puces
de Clignancourt* (Clignancourt Flea Market)
and Tearooms.

Musée de la Poupée (Doll Museum): If you are after a girls' day out, try the *Musée de la Poupée*, located almost around the corner from the Pompidou Center (which Parisians commonly refer to as the "Beaubourg"). Four hundred dolls, dating from 1800 to the present, are housed in this elaborate and enchanting museum. Tucked away on a tiny dead-end street, the museum is a stroll through fashions of the last two centuries. Even Barbie is included. There is also a doll hospital, where people can bring in a doll to be repaired and a small shop where one can buy dolls, doll clothes and doll furniture.

> **Musée de la Poupée,** Impasse Berthaud, (near 22 rue Beaubourg) 3ᵉ. MÉTRO: RAMBUTEAU. BUS: 29, 38, 47 TEL: 01 42 727 311
HOURS: TUE TO SUN, 10 A.M. TO 6 P.M. CLOSED ON MON AND HOLIDAYS
www.museedelapoupeeparis.com/info-autre-lien/infoen.html
TICKETS: €6.50 FOR ADULTS, €3 FOR CHILDREN AGES THREE TO 18

Wheelchair ramps are also available (the museum is listed under "Tourisme et Handicap" for hearing- and mobility-impaired visitors). Strollers are welcome, when the crowd isn't too big. Otherwise, leave them at the entrance. Restrooms are available, but no changing table. Closed on Mondays.

For more doll action, see **Shopping** for *Pain D'Epices,* another sophisticated and tailored doll shop.

Opéra Garnier: If you have a budding ballerina in the family, a performance at *Opéra Garnier* would be an experience of a lifetime. Despite its name, this theater is now the official home of the Paris Ballet. The **Palais Garnier** (Garnier Palace) was also the real-life setting for some of Edgar Degas's famous ballet paintings. And where do you think you can see some of his original work in Paris? Inside the building, the grand staircase and the foyer are simply magnificent, resplendent in velvet, gold leaf, nymphs and cherubs. In 1964, Marc Chagall frescoed the ceiling from which hangs the huge (over six-ton) crystal chandelier. Among the fabulous decorative elements, you will also find several outstanding paintings illustrating the history of opera and ballet from the 18th century to the present, especially through portraits of famous singers, dancers and composers. The *Opéra Garnier* was also the inspiration for Gaston Leroux's Phantom of the Opera. It is said that the Phantom still lurks there—for those with wild imaginations. What about you? And yes, there really is a Box 5. Guided tours are available, but they don't provide the magic of a real-life performance. For children aged four to six, there are "Phantom of the Opera" guides that take visitors around the theater and tell stories about the theater's history. Other activities for children: *visites ateliers jeune publique* (tour/workshops for children) are held on Wednesday afternoons, in French only, for children aged four to six. For children aged six to 10 and seven to 12, there are plenty of artists' workshops and opera costume-making sessions to attend.

Bonus: Beehives on the roof provide honey that is sold in the Opera Bastille shop.

> **Opéra Garnier,** 8 rue Scribe, 9ᵉ
MÉTRO: OPERA.
TEL: 01 40 011 988
HOURS: 10 A.M. TO 5 P.M. DAILY
WWW.OPERADEPARIS.FR
DAILY TOURS IN ENGLISH AT 11:30 A.M. AND 2:00 P.M.

Musée de l'Eventail (Fan Museum): This tiny, yet adorable, fan museum is located on the 3ʳᵈ floor of an apartment building. There are fans dating from the 17ᵗʰ-century to present day, meaning some are over 200 years old. The museum doubles as the atelier of Anne Hoguet, the last fan maker in France, who will also answer questions, restore your old fan, or even make one for you.

> **Musée de l'éventail,** Atelier Hoguet, 2 blvd de Strasbourg, 10ᵉ
MÉTRO: STRASBOURG-SAINT-DENIS
BUS: 38, 39, 47
TEL: 01 42 081 989
HOURS: TUESDAYS 2 P.M. TO 5P.M.,

CLOSED WED TO MON, BANK HOLIDAYS AND AUGUST
www.paris.org/Musees/Eventail/info.html

Musée de la Mode et du Costume (Museum of Fashion): This museum contains almost 100,000 items of clothing, jewelry and professional uniforms, dating from 1735 to the present day. It's housed in a lovely Italian-style palace built between 1878 and 1894. The museum exhibits are displayed in rotation, with two major exhibitions each year. They can showcase a particular couturier's career or explore a single theme.

> **Musée de la Mode et du Costume,** Palais Galliéra, 10 av Pierre-Iᵉʳ-de-Serbie, 16ᵉ
MÉTRO: IÉNA, ALMA-MARCEAU
BUS: 32, 63, 92
TEL: 01 47 208 523
HOURS: 10 A.M. TO 5:40 P.M., CLOSED MONDAYS, NEW YEAR'S DAY AND CHRISTMAS DAY
www.paris.org/Musees/Costume/info.html

After a visit here, be sure to checkout the Yves St. Laurent Museum, located just down the street.

Yves St. Laurent Museum, 10 av Pierre-1ᵉʳ-de-Serbie, 16ᵉ
MÉTRO: IENA
TEL: 01 47 20 85 23
HOURS: DAILY 10 A.M. TO 6 P.M. CLOSED ON MONDAYS AND PUBLIC HOLIDAYS.

FASHION SHOWS

Attend a Paris fashion show at *Printemps*, one of the top three department stores in Paris. Top runway models can be found here flaunting the latest fashions. Shows are held (free of charge) every Tuesday at 10 a.m. on the 7th floor of *Printemps de la Mode*.

> Printemps de la Mode,
64 blvd Haussmann, 9e
MÉTRO: HAVRE CAUMARTIN
TEL: 01 42 82 50 00
HOURS: MON TO SAT 9:30 A.M. TO
7 P.M. AND UNTIL 10 PM. ON SAT
www.printemps.fr

The *Galeries Lafayette* also plays host to fashion shows. These take place on Tuesdays and Fridays at 11 a.m. during the summer.

> Galeries Lafayette,
40 blvd Haussmann, 9e
MÉTRO: CHAUSSÉE D'ANTIN
TEL: 01 42 823 456; OR RESERVE WITH
THE ENGLISH-SPEAKING SWITCHBOARD
OPERATOR AT 01 48 740 230
HOURS: MON TO SAT 9:30 A.M. TO
7:30 P.M. AND UNTIL 9 P.M. ON THU;
CLOSED ON SUNDAYS
www.galerieslafayette.com

Cooking Schools (See *L'Atelier des Chefs* listing under **Mother and Baby Pampering**) Also see the **Hotel Ritz** listing under **Sleeps**.

Marché Aux Puces de Clignancourt (Clignancourt Flea Market): If you've been bitten by the flea market bug, and need to get your fix, this is the place. Many designers and famous faces from all over the world hunt for treasures here, at one of the largest flea markets in Europe. It's filled with thousands of vendors and probably twice as many buyers.

> Marché aux Puces de Clignancourt, av de la Porte de Clignancourt, 18e
MÉTRO: PORTE DE CLIGNANCOURT
BUS: 56, 85, 155, OR 166
TEL: NO PHONE
HOURS: SAT, SUN, AND MON: 8 A.M.
TO 7 P.M.
www.marchesauxpuces.fr

TEAROOM AND SHOPPING SPREE

Ladurée is a quintessentially French tea salon and is the best Paris has to offer. It is conveniently located halfway down the *Avenue des Champs-Elysées*, making it a perfect destination between shopping sprees. Since 1862, it has been offering its signature dessert: macaroons. You can't say you've truly experienced Paris until you've tried at least one. The décor is upscale, so it's best not to visit in jeans or shorts.

Ladurée,
75 av des Champs-Elysées, 8e
MÉTRO: GEORGES V
TEL: 01 40 750 875
HOURS: MON TO SAT 7:30 A.M.
TO 11 P.M.; THE RESTAURANT IS OPEN
7:30 A.M. TO 12:30 A.M.
www.laduree.fr

DUDES

The hot spots for boys out on the town. If climbing Mt. Everest is more what your son(s) had in mind for a visit to Paris, it's not too late—for the workout, that is. For example: there are more than 1,710 stairs to the top of the Eiffel Tower, or 704 steps up to Level Two. There are 385 steps up to the world-famous gargoyles at *Notre-Dame*; about 270 steps up to *Sacré-Cœur* in *Montmartre*; and 284 steps to the top of the *Arc de Triomphe*. For a little less physical bonding experience with your son, consider a visit to *Les Catacombes*, Napoleon's Tomb and the *Musée de l'Armée*. Or for maximum gross-out effect, how about sending a postcard of a sewer rat to your child's best friend? Les Egouts de Paris, the city sewers, is another alternative, which can score your son lots of points with his friends back home.

Les Catacombes, Hôtel National des Invalides, Napoleon's Tomb, *Musée de l'Armée* (Army Museum), *Les Egouts de Paris* (Sewer Museum), Barge Ride on the *Canal St. Martin*, Break dancers in *Les Halles*, *Musée de L'Air et de l'Espace* (Air and Space Museum) and *Musée National de la Marine*

Les Egouts de Paris (Sewer Museum): Just about every kid loves the idea of touring the *égouts* (sewers) in Paris, and it has become a very popular attraction in town. Generally the tour takes an hour, not including the waiting time, especially during the high season, when lines can be quite long. The visit consists of heading underground to visit the museum, then viewing a short film on the history of the sanitation system. Next step is a guided walking tour of the sewers themselves. In the summer, tours are available in English. Most of the tunnels are well-lit, with every tunnel clearly marked with the name of the Parisian street it serves. Street signs are posted just like the street signs above ground. Even pipes from individual buildings have the building names and addresses.

> Les Egouts de Paris,
93 quai d'Orsay, 7ᵉ
Métro: Alma-Marceau
Bus: 42, 63, 80, 92
Tel: 01 53 682 781
Hours: 11 a.m. to 5 p.m.
www.paris-france.org

"Ratatouille", the recently released film about Remy, a rat who dreams of becoming a chef, has made Aurouze, a real-life rat trap shop in the center of Paris, something of a tourist attraction because of one pivotal scene in the movie. Remy's father tells him that humans can't be trusted and to prove his point, he takes him to a shop where dead rats are hanging by strings in the window. There are 21 dead rats, their necks crushed by steel traps, in the shop. They've been a calling card for the business since 1925.

> 8 rue des Halles, 1e
Métro: Les Halles
Bus: 38, 47, 67, 69, 75
Tel: 01 40 411 620
www.aurouze.com

Les Catacombes: A visit to the catacombs of Paris is a must for anyone seeking a ghoulish thrill with a bit of history thrown in (and living to tell the tale to school buddies). It's all skulls and bones here, in what is probably the most macabre place for tourist visits in all of Paris. After infection forced the city to empty its cemeteries (starting in 1786 with the Cemetery of the Innocents in the *Les Halles* area), more than six million skeletons from the Paris cemeteries were moved to the ancient Roman-Gallo quarries. And you can visit them. While the bones were originally thrown pell-mell into the quarries under cover of night (with a procession of priests singing the skeletons away to their new home in the *ossuaire municipal,* (municipal ossuary or house for old bones of the dead), today it is an organized, if macabre scene that meets the visitor. Any kid who loves a good scare will enjoy the shiver down his spine as he gazes at the decorative stacks of skulls, tibias and other bits and bobs of bone arranged in patterns that line the halls under the streets of Paris. Not for the faint-of-heart, nor the youngest visitors. Wear shoes that you don't mind getting dusty and give yourself about an hour for the visit, so arrive well before the 4:00 p.m. closing time. Closed Mondays and some holidays.

Parent's hint: be sure to use one of the outdoor public toilets (very clean) on the street before entering. There are no facilities down in the catacombs. The walk down to this underground graveyard consists of at least 90 steps. No wheelchair or stroller access. Suitable for children aged seven and up.

> Les Catacombes,
1 place Denfert-Rochereau, 14ᵉ
Métro: Denfert-Rochereau
Bus: 38, 68
Tel: 01 43 224 763
Hours: 2 to 4 p.m., Tue to Fri; 9 a.m. to 11 a.m. and 2 p.m. to 4 p.m. Sat to Sun; closed on Mondays and certain holidays
www.catacombes.info

Hôtel National des Invalides is a marvelous memorial that was built by Louis XIV in 1670 to care for soldiers wounded in his service. The grandiose monument—one of the most prominent landmarks in Paris, it also houses Napoleon's ashes. *Les Invalides* (as Parisians prefer to call it) houses three museums: the *Musée de l'Armée,* the *Musée des Plans-Reliefs,* the *Musée de l'Ordre de la Libération.* There are also two churches: *St. Louis* and the *Eglise du Dome.* However, for the dudes in tow, the **Musée de l'Armée** (Army Museum) and **Napoleon's Tomb** will be especially worthy of a visit.

Napoleon's Tomb: In 1840, the body of Napoleon was brought here after the French government received permission from the British government to transport it back from St. Helena to Paris. A hero's funeral was held in Paris for Napoleon, and he was finally buried in the crypt under the *Eglise du Dome,* some 19 years after his death. In the different rooms, you can see his death mask (by Antommarchi); an oil painting by Delaroche, from the time of Napoleon's first banishment (April 1814), showing him with paunch and all; the First Empire exhibit with his field bed and tent; his bedroom as it was at the time of his death on St. Helena; and other souvenirs, such as the hat he wore at Eylau; the sword from his Austerlitz victory, his "Flag of Farewell," which he kissed before departing for Elba, and even his hair and pet dog (stuffed).

Musée de l'Armée (Army Museum) is another popular attraction for the boy who loves strategy and weaponry. This place has a thorough and fascinating collection that will keep any boy riveted, for awhile at least. It's all weapons and armor from the campaigns of Louis XIV, the First World War, the Second World War, and, let's not forget, the Napoleonic wars. There are rooms full of artillery, historic figurines, emblems, paintings, sculptures, drawings, photographs, etc. For parents, the *Cour de Honneur* (Court of Honor) entry, with its cannons, proportion, scale and perspectives, is well worth a visit. Also be sure to see Napoleon's different uniforms—different battle, different uniform—there are over 100,000 uniforms displayed throughout the museum.

Added bonus: One way for a kid to see the museum and leave with a nifty creation is to take advantage of the terrific diversions for children that the museum offers. Visites-Contes (Story Visits) for children age 7 to 12 (in French): kids follow a story based on a character from the museum's collections. Ateliers (Workshops): after visiting the museum, kids create an object from the visit's theme (either Armor and Emblems or Animals). 7- to 12-year-olds make a shield or create a fantastic creature while 9- to 16-year-olds make a poster based on historical posters of war and peace from 1939 to 1945.

> *Hôtel National des Invalides*, Esplanade des Invalides, 7ᵉ
MÉTRO: LA TOUR-MAUBOURG, VARENNES

BUS: 28, 49, 63, 69, 82, 83, 87, 92
TEL: 01 44 425 173
HOURS: 10 A.M. TO 6 P.M. APR TO SEPT; 10 A.M. TO 5 P.M. OCT TO MARCH; CLOSED ON THE FIRST MONDAY OF EACH MONTH AND PUBLIC HOLIDAYS.

> **Napoleon's Tomb** IS OPEN DAILY FROM 10 A.M. TO 5 P.M.
ACTIVITY TIMETABLE: 2 P.M. WED AND SAT.
COST: €6 ADULTS; €4.50 FOR CHILDREN.
www.invalides.org.

BARGE RIDE

Go for a barge ride on the *Canal St. Martin* for only €1.50. This three-hour boat ride heads through nine locks, starting along the *Bassin de la Villette* and ending at *Parc de la Villette*. The barge ride offers amazing views of many of the major historic sites Paris has to offer. Locks can be amazingly slow to fill with water, so be sure to bring along food, drinks and snacks (not available on the barge). Bring extra clothes, too. When gates open, water tends to rush everywhere.

> *Canal St. Martin*,
13 quai de la Loire, La Villette, 19ᵉ
MÉTRO: JACQUES BONSERGENT OR PORTE DE PANTIN.
COST: €1.50

FUN BREAK

In the big underground shopping center of *Les Halles* (pronounced *ley-all*), there is a place where **break dancers** gather together and show off their tips and tricks of the trade to each other. All levels of enthusiasts congregate. Best not to take pictures because most of them are camera-shy. It's right in the heart of Paris, between the *Louvre* and *Notre-Dame*. There's an indoor swimming pool also, and lots of choices for lunch. On top of the mall is a garden where children can practice their newly acquired break-dancing moves.

> **Les Halles** Above the large Les Halles RER métro station, 1^e
MÉTRO: LINES 1, 4, 7, 11 AND 14 LES HALLES, CHATELET
HOURS: 10 A.M. TO 7:30 P.M. MON TO SAT
www.forum-des-halles.com

Musée de L'Air et de l'Espace (Air and Space Museum): For any boy who loves airplanes, this is a must-see. Charles Lindberg landed his *Spirit of St. Louis* at the famous Le Bourget airport. Located 10 km outside Paris, this airport serves as home of the *Musée de L'Air et de l'Espace*, and it's jam-packed with miles and miles of planes from all eras of aviation history. Everything from hot air balloons, to World War II military aircraft (the *Spitfire* and *Mustang* can be found here), and more, including a prototype of the *Concorde*. There are educational activities, children's workshop and a sound and light show. The museum boasts a cafeteria and tours can be given in English.

> **Musée de L'Air et de l'Espace**, Aéroport de Paris Le Bourget
MÉTRO: 7, LA COURNEUVE
BUS: 152 (PORTE DE LA VILLETTE), 350 (GARE DE L'EST)
TEL: 01 49 927 062
RESERVATIONS: 01 49 927 022
HOURS: 10 A.M. TO 5 P.M.
www.mae.org

Musée National de la Marine: Ahoy Matey! Intrepid seafarers can explore the underwater world and embark on virtual expeditions at this maritime museum near the Eiffel Tower. Among the fun exercises, young pirates can look out for ship wrecks and stay alert for any sea monsters. They can also chart the course of the Titanic, learn about maritime life, inventions and mythical heroes.

> **Musée National de la Marine** Palais de Chaillot, 17 place du Trocadéro, 16^e
MÉTRO: TROCADÉRO
TEL: 01 53 656 969
HOURS: 10 A.M. TO 6 P.M.
DAILY, EXCEPT MAY 1; CLOSED TUE
COST: €8; CONCESSIONS €6
www.musee-marine.fr

Musée National d'Histoire Naturelle

Carousels in Montmartre

CO-ED

Have some fun with both guys and dolls. The menu of things to see and do in the City of Light with kids in tow is endless, but if we must – we have picked the top of the list to see and do. Take to the skies: Hot Air Balloon and Helicopter Rides, Paris by bicycle, Listen to Gospel, Ride all the Carousels in town, *Cité des Enfants* (Children's City), *Parc de la Villette, Cité des Sciences et de l'Industrie,* Pony Club de la Villette, *La Géode, Musée Grévin, Musée de la Magie* (Museum of Magic) and *Double Fond.*

Eutelsat Hot Air Balloon

In the *Parc André Citroën,* you can go on a hot-air balloon ride, and it's definitely worth it—although the park itself is not the most child-friendly Paris has to offer. The Parc André Citroën is also only a 15-minute walk from the Eiffel Tower. If your aim is to absorb as many breathtaking and spectacular views as possible of the Eiffel Tower, and of the rest of the city for that matter, then a visit here should definitely be on your to-do list. The hot-air balloon ride is sponsored by **Eutelsat,** and it's supposed to be one of the world's largest. It doesn't actually glide across the city, though: it's tethered to the ground, allowing for a direct ride up—500 feet or more. To get a general idea of the size and capacity of this balloon ride, it can accommodate as many as 30 adults and children. Expect to be floating on up there in the sky, enjoying the view, for about 15 minutes. Not advisable for those

suffering from vertigo or a fear of heights. The hot air balloon can be an interesting alternative to the Eiffel Tower itself, whose lines are notoriously long, especially during summer and holiday periods. The wait for a balloon ride is only about half that of its rival. Since weather conditions play a major part in the feasibility of a ride, a morning visit is a good idea: the wind is stronger and the waiting time shorter. The price for a ride can't be beat, either.

> **Eutelsat Hot Air Balloon Ride,** Parc André Citroën, 2 rue de la Montagne-de-la-Fage, 15e
Métro: Javel-Citroën
Tel: 01 44 262 020
Restrictions: One adult per child for a ride.
Tickets: Adults: €12 weekends, €10 weekdays; children 12 to 17: €10 weekends, €9 weekdays; children 3 to 11: €6 weekends, €5 weekdays; under 3 years of age: free. Rides run every 30 minutes, depending on weather conditions.
www.aeroparis.com

Take to the skies, Part 2:
Try a helicopter tour of Paris and Versailles with **French Adventures.** A visit to the *Musée de l'Air et de l'Espace* is included in the package. Flights last 45 minutes, and are available from Tuesday to Sunday from the Paris heliport. On your return flight, you fly over the Palace of Versailles. They also offer a special children's tour of Paris.
> French Adventures, Pick-up location depends on destination
TEL: 01 64 210 268
COST: €350 FOR ADULTS; €300 FOR CHILDREN.
www.frenchadventures.com

PARIS BY BICYCLE
Rent a bike on an early Sunday morning and take a ride along the banks of the Seine—it is the one day of the week when cars are not allowed along the normally busy quays. Bicycle rental and English tour guides available from *Paris à vélo c'est sympa!* Recently, this company was awarded the *Grand Prix du Tourisme.* Come prepared to deposit your passport or €250 for a bike.
> *Paris à vélo c'est sympa!*
Rue Alphonse Baudin, 11e
MÉTRO: RICHARD LENOIR, LINE 5
TEL: 01 48 876 001
HOURS: MON TO FRI. 9:30 A.M. TO 1 P.M. AND 2 P.M. TO 5:30 P.M.; 9:30 A.M. TO 1 P.M AND 2 P.M. TO 6 P.M SAT AND SUN; CLOSED ON TUE

COST: FROM €10 FOR HALF-DAY AND €17 FOR 24 HOURS.
www.parisvelosympa.com/GB/index.html

LISTEN TO GOSPEL
Gospel Dream holds concerts at different times of day and in different churches around the city. The singers and musicians, in particular the trumpet players, are very well-regarded in town.
> Gospel Dream
Location varies; call for timings
TEL: 01 43 140 810 FOR RESERVATIONS
www.gospeldream.com

RIDE ALL THE CAROUSELS IN TOWN
For younger children, it's a favorite Parisian pastime and the whispered "wows" from your little loved ones will be 20 times more fun while watching them go round 'n' round. Carousels can be found in the following locations: *Jardin des Tuileries, Jardin Luxembourg, Jardin des Plantes,* the top floor of the *Forum Des Halles,* at the bottom of the hill of *Sacré-Cœur* in *Montmartre* and at the *Jardin d'Acclimation.*
> *Jardin des Tuileries,* Bordering place de la Concorde, 8e
MÉTRO: TUILERIES OR CONCORDE
TEL: 01 40 209 043
> *Jardin du Luxembourg,* boulevard Saint-Michel
MÉTRO: ODÉON
TEL: 01 42 342 023

> Natural History Museum
(Jardin des Plantes) 57, rue Cuvier, 5ᵉ
MÉTRO: GARE D'AUSTERLITZ, JUSSIEU OR PLACE MONGE
TEL: 01 40 793 000
HOURS: 8 A.M. TO 6:15 P.M. DAILY
COST: FREE ADMISSION

> *Jardin d'enfants des Halles*
(Forum des Halles)
105, rue Rambuteau, 1ᵉ
MÉTRO: CHÂTELET-LES HALLES
TEL: 01 44 769 656
HOURS: 10.AM. TO 7:30 P.M.; PARENTS ARE ALLOWED IN FROM 10 A.M. TO 2 P.M. ON SAT TO SUPERVISE CHILDREN YOUNGER THAN 7.

> *Sacré-Cœur* in *Montmartre*
Place du Parvis-du-Sacré-Cœur, 18ᵉ
MÉTRO: PLACE CLICHY, BLANCHE, PIGALLE, ANVERS, ABBESSES BUS: 30, 31, 60, 80, 85, MONTMARTROBUS (54, 55), 95
TEL: 01 53 418 900
HOURS: CHURCH GROUNDS OPEN 6 A.M. TO 11 P.M.
Bonus: On the bottom of the church on the right are public toilets; tipping required.

> *Jardin d'Acclimatation*,
Bois de Boulogne, 16ᵉ
MÉTRO: LES SABLONS
TEL: 01 40 679 082
HOURS: JUN-SEPT: EVERYDAY 10 A.M. TO 7 P.M. DAILY JUNE TO SPT; 10 A.M. TO 6 P.M. DAILY OCT TO MAY
COST: ADMISSION € 2.50, FREE FOR CHILDREN UNDER 3
www.jardinacclimation.fr
Bonus: Picnic areas and cafes.

Cité des Enfants (Children's City): Nestled in the *Parc de la Villette*, the *Cité des Enfants* is one of the top-notch children's attractions in town. This museum is conveniently located within the incredible *Cité des Sciences et de l'Industrie* (City of Science and Industry) complex. It is a must for hands-on entertainment, offering several attractions spread across the 35-acre family-fun-filled park.

The children's nature and science museum is divided into three enormous discovery zones—one for 3 to 5 year-olds, another for 5 to 12 year-olds and a third area for exhibits. Just about everything in this museum is hands-on. For example, there is a building construction site equipped with hard hats, foam blocks, wheelbarrows, and cranes. Or try the all-time favorite: water cascades where abundant amounts of water falls through water channels and kids can get as wet as they like. Water-proof smocks are available. Older children have the option to work in a make-believe TV studio or to dance on film then see themselves on camera. The nature exhibit includes ant and butterfly farms, a greenhouse and a walk-in anthill. Everything is well-supervised and many of the instructors speak English. Special workshops called

> *Parc de la Villette* (*Cité des Sciences et de l'Industrie* and *Cité des Enfants*), 211 av Jean-Jaurès, 19ᵉ
Métro: Porte de la Villette
Tel: 01 46 915 756
Hours: 10 a.m. to 6 p.m. Tue to Sun
Cost: €5 for a 90-minute session
(children must be accompanied by an adult)
www.la-villette.com

> *Cité des Sciences et de l'Industrie*
30 av Corentin-Cariou, 19ᵉ
Métro: Porte de la Villette Bus: 75, 139, 150, 152, PC1 and PC2, stop: Porte de la Villette
Tel: 01 40 057 000
Cost: Prices vary, free admission with Paris Museum pass
(www.parismuseumpass.fr/flash/hp_en.html)
Hours: 10 a.m. to 6 p.m. Tue to Sun; closed on Mon
www.cite-sciences.fr
Bonus: Strollers and wheelchairs available for loan; several restaurants, ATMs and post office.

> *Cité des Enfants,*
30 av Corentin-Cariou, 19ᵉ
Métro: Porte de la Villette
Bus: 75, 139, 150, 152, PC1 and PC2, stop: Porte de la Villette
Tel: 01 40 057 000
Hours: 10 a.m. to 6 p.m., Tue to Sun; closed Mon. Sessions last 1.5 hours.
Cost: Single price €5 per person. Children must be accompanied by an adult.
www.cite-sciences.fr
Useful information: Two areas: Cité des Enfants (3 to 5 year olds); Cité des Enfants (5 to 12 year olds).

Techno-Cité consist of 90-minute sessions for children 11- to 15 years old. Workshops cover: how to build robots; program video games; or even operate a helicopter. Classes are held on Wednesday, Saturday and school holidays. All classes are in French.

While in the *Parc de la Villette*, be sure to visit the big **La Géode** IMAX 3-D screen, on which you can see the most recent 3-D movies. Of the 11 different gardens within the *Parc de la Villette*, three are especially designed for children. The *Jardin du Dragon* has a slide in the shape of a dragon and a playground. The *Jardin des Brouillards* offers fountains, and in the *Jardin des Dune*, there are windmills that one can pedal. Don't miss the funky and obscure ashtrays and garbage cans designed by the famous designer Philippe Starck.

Pony Club de la Villette offers riding classes and activities for children.

> **Pony Club de la Villette**, *Cité des Sciences et de l'Industrie*
30 av Corentin-Cariou, 19ᵉ
Parc de la Villette
Métro: Porte de la Villette
Bus: 75, 139, 150, 152, PC1 and PC2, stop: Porte de la Villette
Tel: 01 40 058 000
www.cite-sciences.fr

La Géode, located on the South side of the *Cité des Sciences*, houses France's leading movie theater with a projection screen of over 1000 meters.

> **La Géode,** *Cité des Sciences et de l'Industrie* (South side)
29 av Corentin-Cariou, 19ᵉ
Parc de la Villette
Métro: Porte de la Villette
Bus: 75, 139, 150, 152, PC1 and PC2, stop: Porte de la Villette
Tel: 01 40 057 999
Hours: 10:00 a.m. to 9:30 p.m. daily; until 7:30 p.m. Sun; call for performance timings
Cost: €9 for adults over 25; €7 for everyone else

Useful information: In the Café children under 3 are not allowed; 90-minute sessions at 10:30 a.m., 12:30 p.m., 2:30 p.m., and 4:30 p.m. Tues to Sun. Only a limited number of visitors are allowed for each session. No more than two adults per family will be allowed admission. It's best to book tickets the day before, or make this your first visit in the *Parc de la Villette* and get tickets for the first available time slot. Easy-access restrooms throughout the complex; English version headphones are free.

Musée Grévin: There are more than three hundred wax figures of famous people for you to visit here, and you can take pictures with most of them, too. This museum was created in 1882 and has attracted over 45 million visitors since it opened. Be sure to explore some of the popular highlights such as: Louis XIV's grand wedding; Marie Antoinette in prison; the many battle scenes of the Revolution; Louis XVI and his court at Versailles; Neil Armstrong's first step on the moon; and lots more. There are also dozens of entertainers from the worlds of fashion, film, music and television. Music celebrities include: Madonna, Celine Dion, Britney Spears, Elton John and Elvis Presley; while you can see film stars such as: Harrison Ford, Julia Roberts and Bruce Willis. And let's not forget: historical figures, writers, and artists—just about everyone can be found here from Mahatma Gandhi to John Paul II to Albert Einstein to Alfred Hitchcock to your friendly neighborhood Spiderman.

For kids: be sure to take the Grévin's Discovery Tour, which reveals the hidden secrets on how wax figures are actually made.

Children will be allowed to touch and feel wax, resins, the eyes and hair of wax figures. Also included in this program is the Story Time session, where presenters are dressed as knights or princesses and lead your *très mignons* children on a tour of the museum.

> *Musée Grévin,*

10 boulevard Montmartre, 9ᵉ

MÉTRO: RUE MONTMARTRE LINES 8 AND 9

BUS 24, 74, 39

TEL: 01 47 708 505

HOURS: 10 A.M. TO 7 P.M. DAILY

COST: €15.90 FOR ADULTS; €9.15 FOR CHILDREN UNDER 14

www.musee-grevin.com

Grévin's Discovery Tour and Story Time

> *Musée Grévin,*

10 boulevard Montmartre, 9ᵉ

MÉTRO: RUE MONTMARTRE LINES 8 AND 9

BUS 24, 74, 39

TEL: 01 47 708 505 (CALLS WILL ONLY BE ANSWERED 9:30 A.M. TO 12:30 P.M. AND 2:30 P.M. TO 4:30 P.M. MON TO FRI)

HOURS: 10 A.M. TO 6:30 P.M. MON TO FRI; 10 A.M. TO 7 P.M. SAT, SUN AND HOLIDAYS

COST: €15; PROGRAM LASTS 2 HOURS

While there, also check out the completely renovated **Palais des Mirages,** reopened in June 2006. This sound-and-light show was first created for the 1900 World's Fair and has been wowing audiences ever since.

> *Palais des Mirages*
Musée Grévin,

10 boulevard Montmartre, 9ᵉ

MÉTRO: RUE MONTMARTRE LINES 8 AND 9

BUS 24, 74, 39

TEL: 01 47 708 505

HOURS: 10 A.M. TO 6:30 P.M.

MON TO FRI; 10 A.M. TO 7 P.M.

SAT, SUN AND HOLIDAYS

COST: €18 ADULTS; €10.50 CHILDREN 6 TO 14; FREE FOR UNDER 6

Musée de la Magie (Museum of Magic): Set in a creepy vaulted cellar, the world of illusion seems to come alive through magic tricks, robots and interactive games. It's hard to tell what's real or not at this hands-on museum, where there is even an in-house magician. In fact, all the staff members are trained magicians. The language doesn't present too much of a barrier and the audience participation is contagious. English speaking guides are available. On Saturdays, the museum offers the **Ecole de Magic** (Magic School) for children 12 years or older, and adults can join in the fun, too. There are beginner and advanced classes offered. During school holidays, there are workshops for children aged 7 to 12 years old. Workshops include a tour and visit to the museum, lessons in magic tricks, a light lunch and a performance just for parents. All classes are held in French. See **Shopping** to find out where to stock up on magician memorabilia and all things magical.

> ***Musée de la Magie,***
11 rue St. Paul, 4ᵉ
Métro: St-Paul, Sully-Morland
Tel: 01 42 721 326
Hours: 2 p.m. to 7 p.m. Wed, Sat and Sun;
2 p.m. to 7 p.m. daily during half-term,
Christmas and Easter holidays
www.museedelamagie.com

Double Fond: This cafe-theatre
showcases magic tricks and
audience participation is
encouraged. Guests have been
known to disappear for hours.
(Just kidding.) Enjoy the small
venue where you can sit back
and watch everything happen
right in front you. It's an ideal
place to take the kids when you
need a little down time and they
still need to eat. Try attending
the matinees, where kids are
encouraged to take part in the
act since it is especially designed
for them. Although the entire
program is in French, most of
the performances are based
on traditional and classical-
style card tricks—all hands
and gestures. Sometimes there
are special shows in English,
especially during the holidays. Be
sure to plan ahead. This place is a
bit tricky to find, but worth it.

> ***Double Fond***, 1 place du
Marché-Ste-Catherine, 4ᵉ
Métro: St-Paul
Tel: 01 42 714 020
Hours: 9 p.m. Tue to Sat; extra session
at 11 p.m. July and Aug; performances
lasts 1,5 hours
Cost: €18 for adults;
€13.50 for students
www.doublefond.fr
Useful information: Magic
classes are offered for children
at 4:30 p.m. to 5:30 p.m. on Sat.
Adults and teenagers can get in
on the fun, too.

PLAYGROUND PARADISE

The best fuss-free playgrounds Paris has to offer. Children can linger around the ponds and playgrounds while parents can enjoy yummy *crêpes* and sip their cappuccinos while overlooking the magnificent Parisian landmarks and beyond. *Jardin d'Acclimatation, Jardin des Tuileries*, Toy Sailboats, *L'Enfance de l'Art, Aquaboulevard* and *Parc Asterix*.

Jardin d'Acclimatation
(Zoological Gardens). If the
Luxembourg, Tuilerie, and
Champs-de-Mars pony rides,
carousels, swings, jungle gyms
and ice-creams didn't satisfy
your child, consider a trip to the
Jardin d'Acclimatation on the
edge of the *Bois de Boulogne.*
The **Bois de Boulogne** is sort of
the equivalent to Central Park
in New York City. The *Jardin
d'Acclimatation* was a gift from
Napoleon III in 1860. Back then,
exotic animals—camels, bears,
a giraffe and more roamed
the grounds until they were
eaten for New Year's Eve dinner
in 1870 at the height of the
Paris famine. Since 1900, the
park has combined education
with outright fun. It is *au naturel*
Disney meets Toys R' Us: more
than just a playground, it is an
amusement park with all the
trimmings. Start your visit by
catching **"Le Petit Train"** (the Little
Train), which comes chugging
along every 10 minutes at *Porte
Maillot.* Be sure to purchase a
round-trip fare with your entry
fee to the park, you will save
an extra €1.50. The train ride
provides parents and children
a short-cut into the park, and
it's highly recommended.
Otherwise, you face a bit of a
hike into the actual park itself,
and if you plan to spend at least
half a day here, the extra fare
is worth it, especially at the
end of the day. There is also a
special section on the train to put
strollers, diaper bags, etc.

> **Jardin d'Acclimatation,**
Bois de Boulogne, 16ᵉ
MÉTRO: LES SABLONS
TEL: 01 40 679 082
HOURS: 10 A.M. TO 7 P.M. DAILY JUNE TO
SEPT; 10 A.M. TO 6 P.M. DAILY OCT TO MAY
COST: €2.50, FREE FOR CHILDREN UNDER 3
www.jardinacclimation.fr

> **Le Petit Train** at *Porte Maillot*
(next to the restaurant l'Orée
du Bois).
TRAIN DEPARTS EVERY 20 MINUTES.
COST: €5 FOR A ROUND-TRIP TICKET

Useful information: Map of the
grounds is located inside the gate.

While in the park, be sure to
explore several attractions such
as the **La Rivière Enchantée**
(Enchanted River), a mechanized
boat ride; the **Musée en Herbe**
(Outdoor Museum); the games,
including real bowling; the
mechanical, self-operated boats;
music, marionettes, trampolines,
water fountains, playgrounds
and mini-golf; the **Explor@dome**;
La Petite Ferme (Little Farm);
and the **Miroirs Déformants**
(Fun House of Mirrors). It is
definitely a full day's worth of
fun, and is bursting with activity
for toddlers and older kiddies.
It is also rated as the best park

in Paris. There are a number of food options, from quiches to grilled meat and picnic grounds are available. There are many restrooms with changing tables. Be sure to bring along bathing suits for hot summer days.

Jardin des Tuileries (Tuileries Gardens): In addition to the two huge parks that border Paris (the *Bois de Boulogne* and the *Bois de Vincennes*), a good option within the city is the 24-hectare *Jardin des Tuileries* between *rue de Rivoli* and the *quai des Tuileries* on the Right Bank. It's the city's oldest park. Similar to the *Jardin du Luxembourg*, there are playgrounds, toy boat rentals, pony rides, skateboard and rollerblade practice areas, a puppet theatre, cafés, and a carousel. But there are also several trampolines (northwest corner) and a very cool playground with unusual equipment for climbing, jumping and riding. In the winter, an open-air ice skating rink is an option, too. Be sure to look out for sculptures by Rodin, Giacometti, Maillot and Roy Lichtenstein, to name a few.

> **Jardin des Tuileries,**
Bordering Place de la Concorde
MÉTRO: TUILERIES OR CONCORDE
TEL: 01 40 209 043
HOURS: DAILY 7:30 A.M. TO 7 P.M.
COST: FREE

Orientation: If you stand at the reflecting pond, you'll be standing along the Grand Axis. Look East and you'll see that it aligns with the arch of the *Place du Carrousel*, the *Pyramide du Louvre*, and the *Cour Carrée* (Square Courtyard) of the Louvre Museum. Look West and you'll see that it aligns with the *La Place de la Concorde* obelisk, the *Arc de Triomphe* and the *Grande Arche de la Defense*. Paris is indeed a city of perspectives. The Tuileries, now a garden that attracts children, lovers, daydreamers and ordinary folks, was once a palace, a prison and the site of the first and second Communes.

Jardin d'Acclimatation

Jardin d'Acclimatation

Marie-Antoinette and her family lost the monarchy here—and later lost their heads at the *Place de la Concorde*—and more than 1000 people were slaughtered in the palace during the French Revolution. A few years later, Napoleon lost the castle and it was left a burned-out shell. **Bonus:** There's a trampoline kids can bounce on. Tickets are €2 for a five-minute turn; €15 for 10 tickets.

During the summer months of July and August and at Christmas time as well, a fun fair runs along the northern edge of the park, on the rue de Rivoli side. This carnival-style fair is filled with lots of stands offering games, roller coaster rides and a Ferris wheel. The Ferris wheel is the real show stopper—it's h-u-u-u-u-ge. Every winter the **Grande Roue** (Ferris wheel) returns to the *Jardins des Tuileries* at the very bottom of the Champs-Elysées, on the other side of the *Place de la Concorde*. Park restrooms are available for a small fee under the stairs near the *rue de Rivoli Métro* (under 12 years, free). Even better, the most wonderful public toilet is located at the Concorde entrance to the Tuileries, just inside the gate; fully equipped, you pay a small fee to use it—and you can buy film, too.

TOY SAILBOATS

These can be rented on Wednesdays, weekends and school holidays. The sailboats are not battery-operated; they are miniature schooners that sail across the ponds with just a push of a stick. The same sailboats can be found in the *Jardin du Luxembourg.*

Workshops: *L'Enfance de l'Art* (The Childhood of Art) holds 90-minute workshops in art and gardening for children ages 4-12. Classes are held in French.

> ***L'Enfance de l'Art***
Between Place de la Concorde and Le Louvre, 1ᵉ
MÉTRO: BIR HAKEIM, TROCADERO
TEL: 01 42 961 933
www.lenfancedelart.com

Aquaboulevard: Set in tropical lush surroundings, this indoor-outdoor water park is open year-round and it is a favorite with children of all ages. It also happens to be Europe's biggest water park, offering a wide variety of thrills and loads of fun activities. Kids can surf in the indoor wave pools—a loud horn sounds to let everyone know the wave machine is about to turn on. Practice surfing moves or swim through rivers and waterfalls, splash around the 10 different types of water slides, wade in waterbeds with bubbles and lie on the outdoor beach. And let's not forget about the loads of water play equipment available. Despite the abundance of choices, there are two favorites that can be found here. The first is the tunnels and long slides that send kids splashing into one of the many pools. The other show stopper is the famous Jacques Cousteau whale. It's life-size and hollow, allowing kids to crawl around inside and exit through one of the many water slides. Moms and Dads aren't left of the fun, either. There are steam baths, saunas and Jacuzzis on-hand. During the summer months, from June to August, the outdoor beach and pool area is one of the city's most popular hotspots, and very crowded. Also on site, there is a 14-screen cinema complex, seven restaurants, the Forest Hill fitness club, a 1000-meter sports store, tennis, bowling and a play area. A word to the wise on swimwear: Bermuda shorts for men and boys are NOT allowed.

> *Aquaboulevard*

4-6 rue Louis-Armand, 15ᵉ

Métro: Place Balard

Bus: PC1, 42, 88, Balard

Tel: 01 40 601 515

Hours: 9 a.m. to 11 p.m. Mon to Thurs; 9 a.m. to midnight Fri; 8 a.m. to midnight Sat; and 8 a.m. to 11 p.m. Sunday

Cost: €25 for adults April to Sept; €20 Sept to April; €10 for children 3 to 11 years old; children under 3 not allowed

www.aquaboulevard.com

Parc Astérix: This theme park is named after the cartoon character Asterix, created and drawn by René Goscinny and Albert Uderzo. Asterix and his crew of jolly Gauls are regarded as France's most popular and widely read comic strip characters. The whole family will be entranced with fun-filled activities with a general focus on historical content. And, yes, it's still billed as fun. For example, there are six themed areas within the park: the Gallic village, ancient Rome, ancient Greece, the Middle Ages, the 17ᵗʰ century and modern times. Now, put this all together with the most unbelievable rides Europe has to offer, like Europe's tallest and scariest roller coaster, the *Tonnerre de Zeus* (Zeus's Thunder) and a giant slide called Race de Hourra—and education can't get much more fun. There are slides, roller coasters and dolphin performances, to boot. There's a hotel on the premises.

> *Parc Astérix,* About 23 miles north of Paris. Motorway A1 Paris-Lille, direct exit to Parc Astérix, between exits No. 7 and No. 8.

Métro: Line B3. Get off at Roissy CDG1 and take the Parc Astérix shuttle (platform A3).

Tel: From France: 08 26 301 040 From abroad: 011 33 3 44 623 131

Hours: Opening times vary according to season; check the Web site or call for details.

www.parcasterix.fr

MOTHER & BABY PAMPERING

Mother and baby-bonding ops, in Paris
and beyond.
*L'Atelier des Chefs, Le Village Joué Club,
Royal-Thalasso Barrière Hôtel Spa* at *La Baule,*
and *Espace Thermal "Evian".*

L'Atelier des Chefs: This school offers cooking classes for both big and little people. *Recent Graine de Chef* (Budding Chef) courses, for kids 7 and up, give them lessons in making raspberry ice cream sodas, mousse au chocolat and *Cake à la Vache qui Rit et aux courgettes* (savory cheese and zucchini bread). Menus and dates vary. Birthday parties (make the cake and eat it) are available for children 7 and up (limit 10 kids). There are three locations, in the 8e, 9e and 20e arrondissements. Reservations highly advisable.

> *L'Atelier des Chefs*

10 rue de Penthièvre, 8^e
(5 minutes from Champs-Elysées)
MÉTRO: LINES 9 AND 13, MIROMESNIL
BUS: 22, 28, 32, 43, 52, 80, 84, 93
TEL: 01 53 300 582
www.atelierdeschefs.com

Le Village JouéClub: A kid's paradise in the Passage des Princes—2000 square meters of toys, toys, toys plus theatrical and musical performances; Coup'kid—a child-friendly hair salon; birthday parties; Canal J (children's television); and a reservation desk for performances around Paris. Toys are spread over the two floors at individual brand boutiques scattered throughout. It's magical. Just try to get out without buying something. There's a restroom with a changing table on ground floor.

> *Le Village JouéClub*

3/5 blvd des Italiens, 2^e
MÉTRO: RICHELIEU, DROUOT
BUS: 32, 42, 67, 74, 85
HOURS: 10 TO 8 P.M. MON TO SAT; CLOSED SUN
TEL: 01 53 454 141
www.villagejoueclub.com

Royal-Thalasso Barrière Hôtel SPA at *La Baule:* Leave the mobile phone, computer, Blackberry, Palm and anything else that might take you out of this pampered world home. In just three hours (from Paris), you and your baby (and children up to four years old) can receive the ultimate special treatment in this gorgeous setting in the Brittany region of France. The Belle Epoch hotel, built in 1896 and situated on the Bay of *La Baule*, offers a variety of "cures." A six-day visit with your new baby comprises three individual treatments and three group sessions (in the pool, for example), plus a beauty session and a visit with a gynecologist. Other possibilities exist for the mother with a baby under nine months—*and* no matter which treatment program you choose, there's a "Petit Club" to entertain your up-to-four-year-old children while you are massaged, hosed down, steamed and soaked. Evening baby-sitting is available (ask the Concierge to arrange it). Don't miss the slimming cure and look into the Spa's short-stay packages. Reservations are an absolute must.

> Royal-Thalasso Barrière Hôtel SPA at La Baule

Royal-Thalasso Barrière,
6 av Pierre Loti, 44504 La Baule
TRAINS: GARE MONTPARNASSE
(www.voyage-snf.com)
TEL: 02 40 114 848
COST: €440 AND UP
www.lucienbarriere.com

Evian: Another great mother-and-baby-pampering spa to visit is Evian. Yes it's the same folks who provide the world's favorite mineral water. **The Espace Thermal Evian** offers an elaborate week of treatments for both you and your baby, including a special bonding and recovery program for mother and child. The program offers everything from Mommy and Baby massages to baby swimming lessons to body scrubs, facials, hydrotherapy cure, and aqua gym and of course, loads and loads of beauty treatments using Evian water. The on-location nannies do all the work for you, dressing, changing diapers, sterilizing bottles, etc., etc...

Try staying at the **Royal Park Evian,** a 42-acre estate at the foot of the Alps on the southern shores of Lake Geneva. Just about every room offers a stunning view of Lake Geneva. Just like the nannies at Evian, the people at Royal Park Evian will equip your room with all the baby necessities a mother could ever need, such as a baby-bouncer chair, crib, sterilizer, formula, high chair and even a stroller. The hotel also offers a fantastic kids' club for older children. There's a free minivan service to the Evian spa every day.

Next door is the sister hotel property, **Hôtel Ermitage,** offering slightly less pricey rates with just about the same services and set-up for mothers.

> Espace Thermal Evian

74500 Evian Les Bains
TEL: 33 50 750 230 (1 866
SCHEDULE: DAILY PROGRAM FOR BABIES
3- TO 24 MONTHS OLD. A COMPANION
PROGRAM IS AVAILABLE FOR FATHERS
AND GRANDPARENTS. HEALTH CERTIFICATES
ARE MANDATORY.

> Royal Parc Evian

South bank of Lake Geneva, BP8,
74501 Evian-les-Bains
TEL: 04 50 268 500
www.royalparcevian.com

> Hôtel Ermitage

South bank of Lake Geneva, BP8,
74501 Evian-les-Bains
TEL: 04 50 268 500
www.en.evianroyalresort.com/
page/p-942/art_id-/hotels/
evian_royal_ermitage

Cathédral Notre-Dame

A FAMILY AFFAIR

Museums, aquariums and other monuments the kids won't admit they are actually enjoying. Make it family-fun! *Cathédrale Notre-Dame de Paris, Musée du Quai Branly, Musée Picasso, Musée National d'Histoire Naturelle,* Le Friday Night Fever/Sunday Skate-in with Pari Roller, Rollers et Coquillages, Fat Tire Bike Tours, *Paris Muse* and *Centre Pompidou,* The Rodin Museum, *Ferme de Gally* and *Château de Vaux-Le-Vicomte.*

Cathédrale Notre-Dame de Paris
(Generally known as *"Notre-Dame"*): This is France's most famous cathedral. Commissioned in 1160, it is a masterpiece of Gothic architecture. The magnificent stained-glass rose windows above the main entrance, the flying buttresses supporting the cathedral walls and roof, and the gruesome gargoyles grimacing out over a spectacular view of Paris make this superlative French Gothic cathedral one of the most famous places to visit in the world. Young children might be more interested to know this was the home of Quasimodo, the hero of Victor Hugo's (and Disney's) *Hunchback of Notre-Dame.* It is also a winner for children because there are 380 steps to climb to the top of the north tower. The steps are divided into two sections: the first level has over 250 steps, while the second level has over 120 steps and only a limited number of visitors are allowed at a given time. Children will feel a sense of accomplishment, or just plain tired, once they complete the task. Expect a line at almost any time of day. There is no elevator. Climbing the tower is not suitable for very young children and kids under 12 years old must be accompanied by an adult. However, at the top is yet another timeless, picture-postcard, classic view of the *Seine* and the *Ile de la Cité.*

The south tower contains a great bell, known as *Emmanuel,* which weighs an awesome 13 tons. It is rung only on significant occasions and holidays. There is also a 7,800-pipe organ the size of a bus. Don't forget to keep a bird's eye view for the kestrels that breed in the cathedral's towers.

There is a small park behind the cathedral with swings and handy benches for parents to rest. Do as the Parisians: soak up the atmosphere and relax on the cathedral's front steps while the children run around in the square in front. This square is called the **Place du Parvis Notre-Dame** and it is the exact reference point used on all signposts throughout the country when they give the distance to Paris. Have the kids try to find the bronze *'Kilometre Zero'* marker.

There are guided tours available in English, once a day. Remember: tours are free with the Paris Museum Pass www.parismuseumpass.fr/flash/hp_en.html

> **Cathédrale Notre-Dame de Paris** *(Notre-Dame)*
6 place du Parvis de Notre-Dame, 4ᵉ
MÉTRO: CITÉ
BUS: 21, 24, 27, 38, 47, 85, 96
TEL: 01 42 345 610
HOURS: DAILY 8 A.M. TO 7 P.M.;
TOWERS OPEN DAILY 9:30 A.M. TO 7:30 P.M. APRIL TO JUNE AND SEPT.;
9 A.M. TO 7:30 P.M. WEEKDAYS, 9 A.M. TO

11 P.M. ON WEEKENDS JULY TO AUG; DAILY 10 A.M. TO 5:30 P.M. OCT TO MARCH COST: FREE ADMISSION TO CATHEDRAL; TOWERS €7, CRYPT €3.30.
www.catholique-paris.com

Musée du Quai Branly: Tucked under the Eiffel Tower is the *Musée de Quai Branly* which opened during the summer of 2006. Built at a cost of $295 million, this museum is devoted to non-Western Art, with a collection of over 300,000 works from Africa, Asia, Oceania and the Americas. There are six workshops offered for children on Wednesdays and Saturdays. These can include: Music of Bali, Japanese theater, and African dances. During the summer months, a 500-seat auditorium opens onto an outdoor theater for music and dance performances and just about anything else. Parents can rent a stroller and there's a restaurant on the premises. There's also a children's workshop.

> *Musée de Quai Branly*
37 Quai Branly, 7e
MÉTRO: LINE 9, ALMA MARCEAU, IÉNA
BUS: 42, TOUR EIFFEL; 80, 92, BOSQUET RAPP; 72, MUSÉE ART MODERNE, PALAIS DE TOKYO
TEL: 01 56 617 000
HOURS: 10 A.M. TO 6:30 P.M. TUE TO THURS; OPEN LATE ON THU UNTIL 9:30 P.M.
COST: €8.50 FOR ADULTS; €6 FOR CHILDREN
www.quaibranly.fr

Musée Picasso: Considered to be the largest collection dedicated and devoted to the 20th century's most famous artist, Picasso, this museum is housed in a magnificent 17th-century palace called the *Hôtel Salé*. Its first owner, Aubert de Fontenay, built a huge fortune by being the sole collector of a French tax on salt. After Picasso's death, his collection of paintings, drawings and sculptures, as well as his own private collection of works by Matisse, Douanier Rousseau, Braque, Degas and Cézanne, became the property of the French state in lieu of death taxes. Children will enjoy the child-friendly art within the collection. Have them find the sculpture of an ape whose face is literally made out of a toy car. There is also an outdoor café open during the warmer times of the year. Children's workshops are offered on Sundays, in French only. There's a cafeteria on the premises.

> *Musée Picasso*, *Hôtel Salé*
5 rue de Thorigny, 3e
MÉTRO: FILLES DU CALVAIRE, ST. PAUL
BUS: 29, 69, 96, 75
TEL: 01 42 717 084
HOURS: 9:30 A.M. TO 6 P.M. WED TO MON, APRIL TO SEPT; 9:30 A.M. TO 5:30 P.M. WED TO MON NOV TO MARCH; CLOSED TUE
www.musee-picasso.fr

Musée National d'Histoire Naturelle (National Museum of Natural History): This museum is located inside the *Jardin des Plantes* and is divided into three collections: **La Grande Galerie de l'Evolution** (The Evolution Gallery), **La Galerie de Minéralogie et Géologie** (The Mineralogy and Geology Gallery) and **La Galerie de Paléontologie et d'Anatomie Comparée** (The Paleontology and Comparative Anatomy Gallery). The most popular, and often overcrowded collection, (especially on week-ends during the summer and holiday months), is the Evolution Gallery. The recently completed renovations in this gallery—30 years in the making—have brought it up-to-date, and it is now one of Paris' most ultra-modern venues for families to visit while in Paris. It uses state-of-the art technologies, such as audio and visual displays, interactive games and touch screens, plus amazing sound and lighting effects, and a whole lot more. Don't miss the enormous blue whale hanging from the ceiling—it is the largest animal that has ever lived on earth; the Noah's Ark-like parade of life-sized animals covering the gamut from anteaters to zebras; the infamous pet rhinoceros Louis XV, which has been there since 1793; and the narwhal, with its 6-foot-long ivory tusk. It's like a swimming unicorn.

In the Discovery Room, nature workshops are run for children under 12 years old. Mini-laboratories are available for teenagers. All classes are held in French. The Gallery includes a cafeteria overlooking the balcony; see **Eats** for more information. Giant crystals, hunks of meteorites and an amazing collection of gemstones and rocks can be found in the Mineralogy and Geology Gallery. Massive numbers of bird, dinosaur, hippo, giraffe, monkey and even human skeletons can be found in The Paleontology and Comparative Anatomy Gallery. There are some over-the-top touches: a human skeleton covered with a fig leaf; pickled monkey and human brains; the one-eyed, 'cyclops' cat and chicken; and skeletons of Siamese twins.

While in the *Jardin des Plantes*, be sure to visit the **La Menagerie,** the first zoo in Paris. But don't get too excited: the zoo is small and there are only a handful of animals now, such as century-old turtles, llamas, monkeys, deer and bears. This choice is best for younger children. Otherwise, this place holds nothing in comparison to the zoo in the *Bois de Vincennes*.

> **Musée National d'Histoire Naturelle,** *Jardin des Plantes*, 36 rue Geoffroy-Saint-Hilaire, 5ᵉ
Métro: Jussieu, Austerlitz
Bus: Lines 24, 57, 61, 63, 67, 89, 91
Batobus: Jardin des Plantes

Tel: 01 40 795 601

Hours: 10 a.m. to 6 p.m. Wed to Mon; 10 a.m. to 8 p.m. on Sat; closed Tue and May 1

Cost: €4 to €

www.mnhn.fr

> **La Ménagerie,** *Jardin des Plantes,* rue Cuvier, rue Buffon, rue Geoffroy-Saint-Hilaire, place Valhubert, 5^e

Métro: Austerlitz, Censier Daubenton or Jussieu

Bus: 24, 57, 61, 63, 67, 89, 91

Batobus: Jardin des Plantes

Tel: 01 40 793 794

Hours: 9 a.m. to 5 p.m. daily

Cost: €5 to €7

www.mnhn.fr

Le Friday Night Fever/ Sunday Skate-in with Pari Roller: Believe it or not, that's what they are called and they are definitely events to see while in Paris. At the very least, check out all the participants before they take off. Every Friday night at 10, around 20,000 people meet in front of the *Tour Montparnasse* for a three-hour, 12- to 15-mile, fast-paced cruise around the city. It's an incredibly popular event in Paris for adults and older children—and it's free. A certain level of blading experience is highly recommended. The participants are known to travel at a very f-a-a-a-a-s-t pace and some have a hard time keeping up, even with the support team that includes a hundred or more

volunteer marshals, first aid assistants and an army of police rollerbladers and motorbikes. This event takes all the credit for the successful creation of the country's first rollerblading police force.

> **Pari Roller,** Place Raoul Dautry, 14e between the Montparnasse office tower and the Paris-Montparnasse train station

Métro: Lines 4, 6, 12, 13

Montparnasse Bienvenüe

Bus: 28, 92, 96, 93, 95

Hour: 10 p.m. every Fri

www.pari-roller.com

A slower-paced alternative when traveling *en famille* is a three-hour, family-oriented mini-version of Le Friday Night Fever. This Sunday afternoon skate-in is organized by ***Rollers et Coquillages*** (Skates and Sea Shells), which caters to skating and rollerblading, and just about anything else on wheels. The route changes every other week, and is traffic-free, like its Big Brother, Le Friday Night Fever. Up to 20,000 people take part in this Sunday event, as well.

> ***Rollers et Coquillages***
Place de La Bastille/ Boulevard Bourdon

Métro: Bastille

Bus 20, 29, 65, 69, 76, 86, 87, 91

Tel: 01 44 549 442

Hour: 2:30 p.m. Sundays

www.rollers-coquillages.org

Another wheeled alternative is a bike ride. *Paris Rando Vélo* departs from the *Hôtel de Ville* (City Hall) at 10 p.m. on Fridays. A different itinerary is planned every other week for this free event. The pace is about 10 kilometers per hour for a total of about 25 kilometers. Bicycles can be hired at the *Forum des Halles* and must be returned during the morning.

> *Paris Rando Vélo,* *Hôtel de Ville* 29 rue de Rivoli, 4ᵉ
MÉTRO: LINES 1, 11 HÔTEL DE VILLE
BUS: 72
HOUR: 10 P.M. FRIDAYS
www.parisrandovelo.com

> *Forum des Halles,* Above the large *Les Halles* RER métro station
MÉTRO: LINES 1, 4, 7, 11 AND 14
LES HALLES, CHATELET

Fat Tire Bike Tours also provides bike rentals and tours around Paris with English speaking guides.

> Fat Tire Bike Tours
Day and night tours meet at the south leg of the Eiffel Tower
MÉTRO: BIR HAKEIM, BUS: 42
TEL: 01 56 58 10 54
COST: €22 FOR CHILDREN; €24 FOR ADULTS FOR DAY TOUR; €26 FOR CHILDREN; €28 FOR ADULTS FOR NIGHT TOUR
www.FatTireBikeToursParis.com

Paris Muse: This company offers the most amazing, high-quality three-hour tours for children aged 6 to 12 at the Louvre. A 2-hour tour includes visits to the Khorsabad Palace, the Egyptian treasures, the Nike of Samothrace and the Mona Lisa— with an additional motivational bit of fun added to the day, called the "Paris Muse Clues." This treasure hunt encourages children to use what they have just learned. The tour offers children clues that lead them to a prize under I.M. Pei's famous glass pyramid. Parents are free to pitch in with solving clues.

> *Paris Muse,* *Musée de Louvre, Palais du Louvre*
MÉTRO: PALAIS ROYAL/MUSÉE DE LOUVRE
BUS: 21, 27, 39, 48, 68, 69, 72, 76, 95
TEL: FROM THE U.S. (011) 33 6 737 733 52; FROM PARIS: 06 73 773 352
COST: €295 PER FAMILY (5 PEOPLE MAXIMUM), WHICH INCLUDES ADMISSION AND THE "PARIS MUSE CLUES" TREASURE: A LOUVRE-RELATED EDUCATIONAL GIFT WITH A €30 VALUE.
www.parismuse.com.

Another sure bet is the *Centre Pompidou,* (*Pompidou* Center), also known as *Beaubourg* Center with its *Galerie des Enfants* (Children's Gallery). The Children's Gallery is dedicated to children and offers two to three exhibits each year. One of the greatest cultural destinations in the world, this museum makes sure kids interact with art in a big way. Guided tours and workshops are held Wednesdays, Saturdays and school holidays for children ages 6-12.

Centre Pompidou

Musée d'Orsay

There are also guided tours for families one Sunday each month. Every Wednesday afternoon, there are films for children ages 7 and up. Reservations are a must! Just about everything is offered in French only.

On the south side of the *Centre Pompidou*, is the colorful and quirky **Fontaine Stravinsky** (Stravinsky Fountain), located, appropriately enough, on *Place Stravinsky*. This fountain was created in 1982-83 by Jean Tinguely and his wife Niki de Saint Phalle. Kids love it. Also be sure to keep an eye on the clock on the north side: *Quartier de l'Horloge*. Every hour, on the hour, the man-size **Le Défenseur du Temps** (Defender of Time) fights off a crab, a dragon or a cockerel. At noon and 5 p.m., he takes on all three. Don't forget to stop in at **Georges:** kids can have something to drink and parents can enjoy a coffee or glass of wine on the outside terrace while observing one of the best views of the city.

> Centre Pompidou
Rue Beaubourg, 4ᵉ
MÉTRO: LINES 1, 11 HOTEL DE VILLE
BUS: 72
TEL: 01 44 781 233
HOURS: 11 A.M. TO 9 P.M. MON, WED – SUN; CLOSED TUE AND MAY 1
CHILDREN'S GALLERY HOURS: 11 A.M. TO 6 P.M. WED TO MON
www.centrepompidou.fr

The Rodin Museum, with its garden sculptures, two sandpits and outdoor café, make it a favorite outdoor stop where the exhausted parent can grab a coffee, or even a salad and a glass of wine, and the excited child can run and jump and stand in awe of "The Gates of Hell" and "The Thinker" and other grand-scale sculptures by Auguste Rodin. As a general rule of thumb: 3- to 5-year olds love the sculptures.

You can also visit the museum in the house, as well. This is not recommended as a wet afternoon activity because most of the fun for kids takes place outdoors.

Parents' hint: download images from the Web site before the visit so the kiddies can recognize the works. It's a sure winner.

> *Musée Rodin*, 77 rue de Varenne, 7ᵉ
MÉTRO: VARENNE, BUS: 69, 82, 87, 92
TEL: 01 44 186 110
HOURS: 9:30 A.M. TO 5:45 P.M. DAILY APRIL TO SEPT; 9;30 A.M. TO 4:45 P.M. DAILY OCT TO MARCH
COST: €6 ADULTS, €4 CHILDREN
www.musee-rodin.fr

Paris Stock Exchange: *L'espace corbeille*, the old trading floor of the Paris stock exchange, is the piece de resistance of guided tours at the *Palais Brongniart*. The tour includes a trip around the 19th-centrury building, including the historic areas of the Stock Exchange, a presentation on the function of the present day stock exchange, and an explanation of the quotation system and simulation of placing a stock order. Tours are available in English and French.

> **Paris Stock Exchange**
Place de la Bourse, 2e
MÉTRO: PLACE DE LA BOURSE
TEL: 01 49 275 555 FOR RESERVATION WHICH IS MANDATORY
HOURS: MON TO FRI 9 A.M. TO 4:30 P.M.; APPROXIMATELY 1.5 HOURS

TICKETS: €5.50 FOR STUDENTS; €8.50 FOR ADULTS
Web site: www.euronext.com (click on "about us" and choose "facilities-Paris")

For a breath of fresh air, city slickers and farmer-wannabes alike will enjoy the *Ferme de Gally* (Gally Farm) in *Saint-Cyr-l'Ecole*, about 30 minutes west of Paris by car. Cooking with flowers, bread making and many other workshops are offered for kids on Wed and Sat, while parents can pick their own fruits, vegetables and flowers. In addition, they've just installed a giant wooden toy play area, a labyrinth, a herb garden and more. The kids can pick their own veggies, too.

Attention: high risk of mud, dirt, chlorophyll, farm animals, sun and fun! Important note: leave the stiletto heels at the hotel and wear a sun hat. Rest and shaded picnic areas available. Strollers will be lost in the labyrinth—bring some sort of baby carrier for the tiny tots.

> *Ferme de Gally,*
RD7 route de Bailly,
78210 Saint-Cyr-L'Ecole
BY CAR: THE FARM IS LOCATED BETWEEN THE TOWNS OF BAILLY AND SAINT-CYR-L'ECOLE. COMING FROM PARIS, TAKE HIGHWAY (AUTOROUTE) A13, TO EXIT NUMBER 6 "ST. GERMAIN-LE CHESNAY". HEAD TO THE LEFT TOWARDS VERSAILLES, AND THEN TO THE RIGHT, TAKING HIGHWAY

D307 towards Bailly. Exit at Bailly, and turn left towards Saint-Cyr-l'Ecole at the first light. Continue two kilometers to the farm. Watch for "Ferme de Gally" signs.

Tel: 01 39 634 800

Hours: 10 a.m. to 12:30 p.m. and 2:00 p.m. to 6 p.m. Wed; 10 a.m. to 6:30 p.m. Sat, Sun and holidays; 10 a.m. to 6:30 p.m. Sat and Sun; 4 p.m. to 5:30 p.m. Mon, Tue, Thu, and Fri for discovering the animals and other activities

Cost: €3.80 for adults; €2.90 for children over 3

www.gally.com

Château de Vaux-Le-Vicomte:

While any first-time visitor to Paris must visit *Versailles*, folks in the know, as well as folks who want to avoid the summer crowds at Versailles, are aware of a nearby alternative which is *Château de Vaux Le Vicomte*. This magnificent 17th-century castle, located outside of Paris, inspired King Louis XIV to such a jealous rage that he arrested the owner and later sentenced him to life imprisonment. King Louis then commissioned the same designers to build *Versailles* for him. In the end, there is not much difference between the two chateaus, other than the size. Both are distinctly marked by the designer and creators. The *Château de Vaux-Le-Vicomte* is like a model of the larger-scale *Versailles*.

The chateau offers an elegant, nighttime, candlelit visit, when more than 2,000 candles are lit all over the grounds and within the chateau itself. A candlelight service is held every Saturday from 8 pm. to midnight. Cost €15.50.

The annual *Dejeuner sur l'Herbe* (Lunch on the Lawn) takes place each June 18. This elegant outdoor event is held in 17th- and 18th-century costume and over 2,000 visitors come dressed in costume. Costumes for adults and children are available on the premises for rent. Admission is free for guests arriving in costumes and a glass of champagne is offered to every guest. Picnic lunches are available for purchase. Musicians play classical music and fencers and baroque dancers partake in the fun. If you miss this event, don't despair: there are several more opportunities during holiday periods, such as Easter, Christmas and New Year. Check the Web site for the full list of prices and more information on these very special events.

> Château de Vaux-Le-Vicomte

Train from Gare de Lyon to Melun takes 55 minutes, then a taxi ride to the grounds. There is also a "Chateaubus" service available on weekend and holidays, for €3.50

Tel: 01 64 144 190

Hours: 10 a.m. to 6 p.m. daily; closed 1 p.m. to 2 p.m. for lunch

Cost: €12.50

www.vaux-le-vicomte.com

IF YOU HAVE TO BE A TOURIST...

Discover the wonderment of all the sight-seeing must-sees Paris has to offer the little ones. It's all about adventure, education, yet playful and artistic fun. *La Tour Fiffel, Arc de Triomphe, Musée d'Orsay, Musée du Louvre, Basilique du Sacre-Cœur, Château de Versailles,* Disneyland® Paris and Walt Disney Studios Park and Diana, Princess of Wales monument.

La Tour Eiffel (The Eiffel Tower): A must-see for any respectable three-year-old and up. Finished in 1889 to celebrate the centenary of the French Revolution, it now represents Paris, if not the entire country. It was the tallest structure in the world when it was built. Strong legs can hike up the 1,710 stairs to get to the top; others can take the elevators (no ramps). The views of Paris are expansive and those who suffer from vertigo are encouraged to not be adventurous. From the top of the tower, you can see for about 50 miles. For the past few years, there has been an ice-skating rink set up on the first platform during winter, offering a great photo-op (skate rentals available).

Postcards can also be mailed from here. The cards can be purchased at the gift shop and the post office is located on the 2nd floor of the tower. This is the only place in Paris that will give your postcards with the *"La Tour Eiffel"* postmark.

Parent's hint: Bring extra sweaters, as the winds can be quite strong and cold at the top of the tower. Also, try to arrive early or visit late in the afternoon to avoid crowds. Another option is a night visit.

The ***Champ-de-Mars,*** the park in which the Eiffel Tower is located, has a playground (at the end furthest away from the Eiffel Tower) that also includes donkey rides, a duck pond, go-carts and lots of green lawns you can actually walk on. There is also a carousel at the foot of the Tower.

> *La Tour Eiffel*, Champ-de-Mars, 7ᵉ

Métro: Bir Hakeim, Bus: 42

Tel: 01 4 411 2 345

Hours: (table from the Eiffel Tower Web site)

www.tour-eiffel.fr

DAILY	LIFT	STEPS
From Jan. 1 to June 15	9:30 a.m. to 11:45 p.m. Final ascension 11:00 p.m. (10:30 p.m. for top floor)	9:30 a.m. to 6:30 p.m. Final admittance 6:00 p.m.
From June 16 to Sept. 2	9:00 a.m. to 12:45 a.m. Final ascension midnight (11:00 p.m. for top floor)	9:00 a.m. to 12:30 a.m. Final admittance midnight
From Sept. 3 to Dec. 31	9:30 a.m. to 11:45 p.m. Final ascension 11:00 p.m. (10:30 p.m. for top floor)	9:30 a.m. to 6:30 p.m. Final admittance 6:00 p.m.

Arc de Triomphe (Triumphal Arch): Commissioned by Napoleon in 1806 to commemorate his military power and achievements, the *Arc de Triomphe* is one of the most recognizable landmarks in the world. It is 50 meters high and 45 meters wide and is located on the top of a small hill called *La Place de l'Etoile* (Star Square) and surrounded by 12 avenues, including the famous *Champs-Elysées*. This memorial arch offers a rooftop terrace with a great view of the city. Be sure to climb the 284 steps to the top and check out yet another amazing view of Paris. Then climb back down and either hop, skip, walk, or run down the *Avenue de Champs-Elysées*, which is located right in front of the arch. DO NOT cross the traffic circle to get to the arch or the *Avenue de Champs-Elysées*; use the **pedestrian tunnel**. If you continue down the *Avenue de Champs-Elysées* for about 300 yards, you end up in front of the entrance gates to the **Jardin des Tuileries.** Continue to the

reflecting pool that offers toy schooners for children, and you will be about 100 feet away from the **Musée du Louvre.** This suggested walk is one of the best strolls in Paris for children and is a stroller-friendly option for parents.

> **Arc de Triomphe**
Place Charles-de-Gaulle, 8ᵉ
MÉTRO: CHARLES-DE-GAULLE-ETOILE
BUS: 73
TEL: 01 55 377 377
www.monum.fr

Arc de Triomphe

Musée d'Orsay (Orsay Museum):
This museum is in the former
Orsay train station, which was
abandoned in the early 1930s.
It sat empty for decades. Under
the threat of demolition, it
was redesigned by architect
Gae Aulenti as a museum. The
original archway of the train
station can still be seen in
addition to the world-famous
clock on the Seine-facing facade.
Try to reserve a coveted table
under the giant clock in the
museum's *Café des Hauteurs*. It
is a great photo opportunity for
the folks back home.

Highlights for the children:
young ballet dancers in-waiting
will love the Degas paintings
located on the third level.
Another big crowd-pleaser
for the under 10 year old set is
Monet. There are also works in
the collection by Renoir, Sisley,
Van Gogh, Gauguin, Seurat
and Signac, to name a few.
Thankfully for tired parents,
all these artists' paintings are
located on the same level of
the museum. And don't miss
the glass floor set over a model
of Paris and the Opera House
neighborhood, located on the
ground floor. It is a different way
to walk all over Paris.
Be sure to pack a pad and
pencil and ask your children to
draw pictures of their favorite
pieces. Alternatively, purchase
postcards in the gift shop of
their favorite pieces of art.

Parent's hint: pick up the free
art-quiz booklet for children
titled, *"Carnets Parcours
Familles"* (available in English.)
Parents should take cues on
what to see and do from this
booklet because the sheer size
of this place is overwhelming,
especially with young children.
There are also 90-minute guided
tours (in French) for children
ages 5-10 years of age. Some
guides can translate into English.
The museum offers strollers for
use, but baby backpacks and
oversized strollers will have to
be checked.

> Musée d'Orsay
1 rue de la Légion d'Honneur, 7ᵉ
Métro: Line 12 Solférino
Bus: 24, 63, 68, 69, 73, 83, 84, 94
Tel: 01 40 494 814
Hours: 9:30 a.m. to 6 p.m. Tue to Sun;
9:30 a.m. to 9:45 p.m. Thu. Tickets sold
until 5 p.m. daily; 9 p.m. on Thu).The
museum is open on Easter Sunday, May 25,
July 14, Nov 1, and Nov 11. It is closed on
Mon and Jan 1, May 1 and Dec 25. Free
admission the first Sunday of each month.
Cost: €7.50 for adults; €5.50 for children
www.musee-orsay.fr

Musée du Louvre: Here, in the
world's largest museum, one in
every seven visitors is American.
More trivia: it would take six
months to visit the entire *Louvre*
if you spent one minute in front
of each piece of work. On your
first visit, you will of course

want to see the museum's No.1 attractions, Leonardo da Vinci's *Mona Lisa*, as well as the iconic *Venus de Milo*. Then take your children to a less crowded area: the Egyptian and Roman antiquities, which receive rave reviews from children. The Louvre has a Web site that can be useful to prepare children for the visit, including a section on visiting for under-18s. It offers information on tours, workshops, special exhibitions and more.

There are several ways to get into the *Louvre*. Even if you have a museum pass, this is one place where there always seems to be a line. An alternative route to enter the museum—although it is not as romantic as entering via the famous glass pyramid—is through the *Galerie du Carrousel,* an indoor shopping mall and food court.

Parent's hint: tickets to the *Louvre* can be ordered in advance from the website and mailed to your home. They give your "priority access" through the *Richelieu* entrance. You pay about an extra €1.10 for each ticket purchased online (double-check for any delivery charges). Remember: under 18s are free, so you only have to purchase tickets for the adults in your group. The first Sunday of each month is also free.

If you have a stroller, you are allowed immediate access into the *Louvre*. Ask any uniformed staff on duty for assistance. Keep in mind that a single gallery visit, followed by lunch, is a lot for a young child. Take a break and head over to the **Jardin des Tuileries.** It is less than 100 yards from the Louvre and filled with child-friendly activities. Be sure to have your hand stamped before leaving the museum, since tickets are valid all-day long. You can head back later in the afternoon for a second viewing.

> **Musée du Louvre,** rue de Rivoli, 1ᵉ
MÉTRO: PALAIS ROYAL MUSÉE DU LOUVRE OR LOUVRE RIVOLI
BUS: 21, 27, 39, 48, 68, 69, 72, 76, 95
TEL: 01 40 205 050
HOURS: 9 A.M. TO 6 P.M. MON, WED-SUN; WED AND FRI UNTIL 9:45 P.M.; CLOSED TUE. FREE ADMISSION THE FIRST SUNDAY OF EACH MONTH AND JULY 14ᵀᴴ
COST: €8.50; FREE FOR VISITORS UNDER 18 YEARS OLD
www.louvre.fr

Basilique du Sacré-Cœur (Sacred-Heart Basilica): It is not on the top 10 list as a favorite for children per se, yet images of the *Basilique du Sacré-Cœur* feature on more postcards than any other Paris site. This whipped-cream, Romano-Byzantine, pure-white basilica, built in 1873, became an instant favorite among Parisians. It took over 12 years to complete. For adults, a visit here will cultivate another one of those Parisian love

Musée du Louvre

affairs, thanks to the spectacular view of the entire city. The fun for kids starts with a ride on the **Funiculaire de Montmarte** cable car, which begins at the *Place St-Pierre* and runs directly to the top of the **Butte de Montmartre** (Montmartre Hill). Métro tickets can be used to pay for the ride. Keep the fun going by climbing all 270 steps to the dome on the roof. Here everyone can enjoy some of the most fantastic views that the city has to offer. Back downstairs, wander the Montmartre neighborhood, including the *Place St. Pierre* with its vintage carousel and the **Place du Tertre,** with its crowds of artists and entertainers eager to sell their wares and showcase their talent. It is, however, a tourist trap with a touch of bohemian creativity. The most popular trinket to take home is a portrait of your child. Be sure to bargain and ALWAYS be aware of pickpockets. Sadly, it is not advisable to visit at night with children in tow.

> **Basilique du Sacré-Cœur**
35 rue du Chevalier-de-la-Barre, 18ᵉ
MÉTRO: ABBESSES, ANVERS, CHÂTEAU ROUGE, LAMARCK-CAULAINCOURT
BUS: 30, 54, 80, 85, MONTMARTROBUS
COST: CHURCH: FREE; €5 CRYPT AND DOME
TEL: 01 53 418 900
www.sacre-coeur-montmartre.com
> **Funiculaire de Montmartre**
DEPARTS DAILY EVERY 5 MIN FROM 6:15 A.M. TO 12:45 A.M.

Château de Versailles: A visit to the *Château de Versailles*—known throughout the world simply as *Versailles*—needs at least a full day to give it any justice. It is a popular destination, with over three million visitors a year—that's about 8,000 folks a day. It is also included on all the tour-group itineraries, and is especially busy on Tuesdays, when many of the museums in Paris are closed. Your best bet is to begin your visit in the early morning. The *Château de Versailles* is the world's most elegant royal chateau. Both the house and the gardens are over-the-top luxurious. However, there are plenty of child-friendly and kid-tested activities to be found. The chateau is straight-forward: the **Galerie des Glaces** (Hall of Mirrors), with its 357 mirrors, is impressive and literally dazzling. The **Salon d'Apollon** (Throne Room) and the **Chambre du Roi** (King's Bedroom) are favorites, too. Outside is where most kid action takes place, though. It's best to tour the park by bicycle which can be rented within the park. Or take the sightseeing train that circles the park. Horse-drawn carriages are always a sure hit, too. And if you are lucky enough to visit during the summer months, you can hire a row boat and cruise along the *Grand Canal*. There is also a small petting zoo where kids ages 5-12 can brush donkeys and feed chickens. Marie Antoinette's full-size toy village—the Queen's Hamlet and the Queen's Cottage—is another winner, but it's a bit of a hike to get there. Audio Guides are available in English. English-language guided tours of the chateau and park are also available. If you speak French, there are tours for children and families, as well as workshops for children. The best time of year to see the gardens is on summer weekends, when jets of water from the fountains dance to the

sound of Baroque music. This show is called les *Grandes Eaux Musicales* (Musical Water), and is only held on Saturdays and Sundays. Also during the summer weekends (July-Sept), there are firework displays called the *Grandes Fêtes de Nuit*. The royal stables have been renovated and riding students from the **Académie du Spectacle Equestre** perform dressage. Admission: open to the public. **Parent's hint:** there are several cafe options for lunch; the restaurant *La Flottille* offers a kids' menu. In the summer, there is an outdoor terrace. Otherwise, a picnic lunch can be a winning option. Children's pushchairs and metal-framed baby carriers are not permitted in the Palace rooms. Children under one year old must be carried in an all-fabric baby sling or front carrier. There are no toilets in the Palace rooms and no changing tables.

> **Château de Versailles**
Town of Versailles
BY TRAIN: THE NEAREST STATION IS VERSAILLES RIVE GAUCHE ON LINE C OF THE RER; THE PALACE IS AN 8-MINUTE WALK AWAY; BY BUS FROM PARIS: TAKE BUS NO. 171 FROM PONT DE SÈVRES MÉTRO STATION; THE BUS STOP IS JUST OPPOSITE THE PALACE.
HOURS: THE PALACE IS OPEN EVERY DAY EXCEPT MON, ON CERTAIN FRENCH PUBLIC HOLIDAYS OR WHEN OFFICIAL CEREMONIES ARE HELD. CHECK THE WEB SITE BEFORE YOU GO TO MAKE SURE YOU WON'T BE

DISAPPOINTED. OPEN DAILY 9 A.M. TO
5:30 P.M. NOV 1 TO APRIL 2; 9 A.M. TO
6:30 P.M. APRIL 3 TO OCT 31
COST: DEPENDS ON THE SEASON. COUNT
ON BETWEEN €10 TO €25 FOR ADULTS, BUT
IT'S FREE WITH A MUSEUM PASS. CHILDREN
UNDER 10 ARE FREE.
www.chateauversailles.fr

**Disneyland® Paris and
Walt Disney Studios Park:** The
lure of Disney is unavoidable for
some when visiting Paris. And
wondering whether to go or not
is a hard decision, for just about
any family. It is only a small trek
from downtown Paris, and it's
open 365 days a year. It's also
Europe's No.1 tourist attraction.
A highly recommended option
is the one-day approach. In this
case, to get the most bang for
the buck, do some advanced
planning. The park is, after all,
one-fifth the size of the entire
city of Paris. Keep in mind that
it's hardly likely you will be able
to visit everything the park has
to offer.

Suggestions for the one-day
approach:

1) Download a park map
from the Disney Web site
(www.disneylandparis.com);

2) Plan to visit only one of the
five park areas. Choose from:
Adventure land, Discovery land,
Fantasyland, Frontierland, Main
Street USA or the new Walt Disney
Studio Park;

3) Be warned: during peak times,
such as summer or French school
holidays, expect the waiting time
for each ride to be on average
70 minutes or longer; 4) Get the
Fastpass®, available on a few, select
rides. The Fastpass® provides
visitors with a designated time for
the ride, and gives them priority
in the line. However, there are
only five Fastpass rides: Space
Mountain: Mission 2, Indiana
Jones® and the Temple of Peril,
Peter Pan's Flight, Big Thunder
Mountain and Star Tours.

A bitter truth about the magical
world of Disney: prices for food are
outrageous. Expect to pay at least
€4.70 for hot dog.

Monsieur and Mademoiselle
Mouse's best travel tips and tricks:

1) Parents of children under 6 years old might want to hold off on a visit to the Magic Kingdom, especially during high season. It's extremely tiring for little ones to wait in line for hours in the heat and sun. It's also expensive— you may well find better ways to entertain your small children in Paris .

2) Lion King Show: Plan to have dinner at least ½ hour before the show starts at the Hyperion Café. Folks wait in line for hours to get tickets, but if you order food in the café where the show takes place, you can get fantastic seats, a good meal, and skip the line for one of the park's top shows.

3) Try to watch the parade from its starting point. Then, while everybody else is waiting to see it pass, you can head over to a ride before the lines begin to form again.

4) Just before the park closes, the lines of many rides get shorter, because lots of people are doing their last minute shopping. It you get lucky, you may be able to hop on a few more rides without the long wait.

5) Book the breakfast with the Disney characters. Kids can meet and greet as well as obtain photographs of their favorite characters. This avoids waiting in lines during the day to get coveted souvenir pictures, so you can spend more time on the rest of the day's activities.

6) **Be advised:** there is no pharmacy on site.

7) Bring your own snacks and water to save some money

> **Disneyland® Paris**
Marne-la-Vallée
BY TRAIN FROM PARIS: IT'S A 40-MINUTE JOURNEY BY THE RER COMMUTER TRAIN, WHICH DROPS YOU OFF ONLY A YARD OR SO AWAY FROM THE ENTRANCE GATES. "ROCK STAR PARKING" COULD NOT GET ANY BETTER.
TEL: 01 60 30 60 53
TICKETS: ON SALE AT MOST HOTELS, MÉTRO STATIONS, THE DISNEY STORE (CHAMPS- ELYSÉES), THE VIRGIN STORE AND THROUGH THE INTERNET.
www.disneylandparis.com

Diana, Princess of Wales monument: Where Princess Diana will always be remembered... The Flame of Liberty "monument"—a full-size, gold leaf-covered replica of the flame carried by the Statue of Liberty—is located on the *Alma Marceau* roundabout, close to the river Seine. Since Princess Diana's car accident was in the tunnel underneath, the flame has become an unofficial pilgrimage point for her admirers.

> **Diana, Princess of Wales monument**
Place de l'Alma, North bank of seine, near Grand Palais, 16ᵉ
MÉTRO: ALMA-MARCEAU
BUS: 42, 63, 80, 92

SLEEPS

Hop in to hip inns that offer real value for money – from affordable to no-frill finds. Discover the right family hotel with ease and comfort.

Four Seasons George V: This world-renowned, five-star hotel group boldly attempts to go one step further in Paris, by offering an almost-unknown child-friendliness. Luxurious and legendary, it pampers its littlest guests with a plethora of services, right down to the child-size bathrobes and bedtime milk and cookies.
> Av George-V, 8^e
TEL: 01 49 527 000
RATES: FROM €750 A NIGHT
www.fourseasons.com

Hotel Mayet: This place is cozy and incredibly child-friendly—right down to the tablecloth and tableware breakfast is served on. Rooms are decorated in an Ikea-meets-Pottery-Barn style, with a bit of French flare thrown in. An ideal place to stay when traveling with older children: although rooms don't connect, there are only five rooms on each floor. Breakfast is included. Closed the month of August and one week during the Christmas holidays.
> 3 rue Mayet, 6^e
TEL 01 47 832 135
RATES: FROM €120 A NIGHT
www.mayet.com

Hotel Le Sainte-Beuve: An adorable and affordable gem located on a small side street just two blocks away from the Luxembourg Gardens—a real find for a stay with children. The hotel reception was designed by famous British interior designer David Hicks.
> 9 rue Sainte-Beuve, 6^e
TEL: 01 45 482 007
RATES: FROM €120
www.hotel-sainte-beuve.fr

The Hotel Ritz: This legendary place for big spenders and movie stars is a Parisian landmark that caters to children as well as grown-ups. While there is no official kids' club, children can enroll in the world-famous Ritz-Escoffier cooking school and start training early for executive chefdom. There are also seasonal family events, like the Easter Family Brunch featuring a massive Easter egg hunt on the terrace of the Cesar Ritz salon, among live rabbits and chicks. In the afternoon, a Ritz pastry chef will instruct families in the art of making chocolate Easter eggs.
> 15 place Vendôme, 1^e
TEL: 01 43 163 030
RATES: FROM €710
www.ritzparis.com

Le Meurice Paris Hotel: If you're looking for a place to spend that year-end bonus, this is the place to lay your tired heads. Located across from Tuileries Garden between Place de Concorde and the Louvre, Le Meurice puts the "P" in pampering for the entire family. Book the Family Program for €1390 a night and both the parents and kids are treated like royalty in their respective adjoining rooms. Upon

check-in, the kids receive child-size bathrobes, slippers, a cuddly stuffed dog, chocolates and a DVD player to use with a selection of DVDs. Also included in the package is 2 carousel rides per child in Tuileries Garden and a treasure hunt around the hotel organized by the concierge. Room amenities for the parents include high-speed internet access, bathrobe and slippers, plasma TV, bar and refrigerator, sitting area, writing desk and twice daily maid service. Did we mention there's also a spa? Every day begins with an American-style breakfast served in the restaurant or in suite. With so much to do at the hotel, you may be praying for a rainy day.
> 228 rue Rivoli, 1e
Tel: 01 44 581 010
Rates from: €795 for rooms with views of Tuileries Garden
www.meuricehotel.com

Hotel de Fleurie: This small three-star hotel has long been a traditional favorite for traveling families: it's affordable and located in great part of town. Children under 12 years of age stay free. There are several connecting rooms and family suites available.
> 32-34 rue Grégoire-de-Tours, 6e
Tel: 01 53 737 000
Rates: Family room from €310 to €360
http://fleurie-hotel-paris.com/

Hotel d'Angleterre: This beautiful three-star hotel was a former British Embassy and has only 27 rooms. It's a real gem, especially due to the location. It is in walking distance of Luxembourg Garden, the *Louvre* and *Notre-Dame* Cathedral. Rooms go quickly for this quiet hotel located just off the *Boulevard de St. Germain* and close to the *Musée D'Orsay*. Ernest Hemingway was a former guest in 1921 (Room 14). There is a courtyard where a complimentary breakfast is served.
> 44 rue Jacob, 6e
Tel: 01 42 603 472
Rates: Suites from €290
www.hotel-dangleterre.com

Hotel Verneuil: While this charming 17th-century hotel is regarded as a well-kept secret mostly because of the friendly ambiance, it is also conveniently located on a private street, just off the *Saint-Germain-des-Près*. Rooms are decorated in a classic style with beautiful marble bathrooms.
> 8 rue de Verneuil, 7e
Tel: 01 42 608 214
Rates: From €210
www.hotelverneuil.com

Hotel Relais Saint Germain: This small, four-star, luxury hotel has a reputation as an oasis on the left bank. Rooms are spacious, and each is meticulously decorated with original oak paneling, exposed beans; stripes, plaids and print tones, for a cozy country-style décor. It is situated near the left bank and located near the *Odéon, Sorbonne*

> 9 Carrefour de L'Odéon, 6ᵉ

Tᴇʟ: 01 43 291 205

Rᴀᴛᴇs: Fʀᴏᴍ €275 ꜰᴏʀ ᴅᴏᴜʙʟᴇ ʀᴏᴏᴍ

www.hotel-paris-relais-saint-germain.com

Mije: Billed as one of the best hostels Paris has to offer, Mije consists of three 17ᵗʰ-century residences. The rooms are clean, simple and use ultra-white linen sheets. Up to eight people can sleep in a room and all rooms have a shower and basin. Downfall: there is a 1 a.m. curfew. While special arrangements can be made, don't count on it. There are restaurant facilities at the Fourcy address, but not at the other locations. The hostel only accepts children over five years of age. Located in the heart of Paris, visitors are steps away from the *Louvre, Les Halles*, Luxembourg Garden, *Bastille* and more.

> 6 rue de Fourcy, 4ᵉ;

> 11 rue du Fauconnier, 4ᵉ;

> 12 rue des Barres, 4ᵉ

Tᴇʟ: 01 42 742 345 (ꜰᴏʀ ᴀʟʟ ᴘʀᴏᴘᴇʀᴛɪᴇs)

Rᴀᴛᴇs: Fʀᴏᴍ €28 ᴘᴇʀ ᴘᴇʀsᴏɴ

www.mije.com

Meridien Montparnasse: Not only is this hotel located just minutes away from the Eiffel Tower, but it also offers the best American-style breakfast in town, included in the room rate. Children have such a wide variety of breakfast choices, they could never go away unfulfilled.

Added bonus: the size of the guest rooms are among the most generous Paris has to offer. During high season, this hotel offers a Baby Brunch, including clowns and an in-house fun fair, specifically catered to children.

> Rue du Commandant Mouchotte, 19ᵉ

Tᴇʟ: 01 44 364 436

Rᴀᴛᴇs: Fʀᴏᴍ €465

http://starwoodhotels.com/lemeridien

Millesime Hotel: This small, luxurious and charming 17ᵗʰ-century hotel was refurbished a few years ago and has established itself as an ideal home away from home. Several rooms look out over the lovely courtyard.

> 15 rue Jacob, 6ᵉ

Tᴇʟ: 01 44 079 797

Rᴀᴛᴇs: Fʀᴏᴍ €380 ꜰᴏʀ sᴜɪᴛᴇs

www.latinquarter-paris-hotel.com

Palais Bourbon: This two-star hotel can accommodate a family of four in a suite. Rates include breakfast. There are a few rooms available with a nice view of the Eiffel Tower.

> 49 rue de Bourgogne, 7ᵉ

Tᴇʟ: 01 44 113 070

Rᴀᴛᴇs: Fʀᴏᴍ €162 ꜰᴏʀ sᴜᴘᴇʀɪᴏʀ ǫᴜᴀᴅʀᴜᴘʟᴇ ʀᴏᴏᴍ

www.hotel-palais-bourbon.com

Hilton Paris: Always a reliable favorite, especially with Executive Lounge access, where children can load up on freebies such as bottled water, soft drinks, snacks, etc. Close to the airport, yet a stone's throw away from all the major Parisian attractions.
> 18 av de Suffren, 15ᵉ
TEL: 01 44 385 600
RATES: FROM €559
www.hilton.com

Relais Christine: Near the Louvre and Notre Dame, in the center of St.-Germain-des-Près, is a 16th-century mansion converted into a 51-room hotel. Some of the suites have terraces that over a lovely garden blooming with flowers. There's also a nice courtyard.
> 3 rue Christine, 6e
TEL: 01 40 516 080
RATES: FROM €345 FOR DOUBLES
www.relais-christine.com

Hotel Scribe: Initially built as a private mansion for a wealthy banking family, it is now considered the crown jewel of the Sofitel hotel chain. Recently refurnished and redecorated, this four-star hotel offers apartments that have a separate entrance and can come equipped with a registered nanny. The hotel is located between the *Opera Garnier* and *Place Vendôme*.
> rue Scribe, 9ᵉ
TEL: 01 44 712 424

RATES: FROM €260 FOR NO CHANGE/CANCELLATION
www.sofitel.com

Business Hotels: Another option to consider for overnight stays is business hotels, such as Ibis, Mercure, Sofitel and Novotel, all owned by the Accor group. Collectively this hotel group consists of over 159 hotels throughout Paris, including all service-level categories (stars). If you have a child who is old enough for a collapsible umbrella stroller and a few *métro* steps, look into some of the locations in the outer arrondissements: since the high season for tourists is the low season for business travelers, you can find some surprising deals. Many of these hotels allow one or two children under the age of 11 to stay for free, and they often have a fold-out bed or trundle that converts back to a sofa during the day. They also usually have a good, kid-friendly restaurant on the premises, so you can eat early and get the kids to bed—a big plus after a long day of sight-seeing.
> www.accor.com

Short-term apartment rental: Just France specializes in apartment rentals in the heart of historical Paris, for short- and long-term vacation rentals. Neighborhoods include the

Ile Saint-Louis, Marais, Saint-Germain des Près, Latin Quarter, *Notre-Dame, Champs-Elysées* and *Montmartre.*
> 800 Lancaster av, Suite M-3, Berwyn, PA 19312
TEL: (610) 407-9633
www.justfrance.com

Paris Luxury Rentals: Luxury vacation apartment rentals are offered in the most exclusive Paris neighborhoods. Apartments are for short-term rental by the week or month.
> 264 28th Street, San Francisco, CA 94131
TEL: TOLL FREE WITHIN THE U.S.: (866) 437-2623 OR (415) 642-1111
www.ParisLuxuryRentals.com

Paris Perfect: This company specializes in rentals of a wide selection of luxury apartments located primarily near major landmarks as well as in upscale neighborhoods.
> 30 Launceston Place, London, England W8 5RN
TEL: (415) 287-3397 IN THE U.S.
www.parisperfect.com

Ville et Village: Offers a selection of private apartments centrally located in Paris. Properties are all personally selected by the staff.
> 2124 Kittredge Street, Suite 200, Berkeley, CA 94704
TEL: (510) 559-8080 WITHIN THE U.S
www.villeetvillage.com

Paris Attitude: Specializes in luxury rentals of centrally located furnished flats. The Web site offers a lot of choices complemented with color photos of the apartment. The agency takes a fee of €210 and half of the rental fee is paid via credit card once the rental agreement is signed, with the rest of the payment due in cash on the date you take arrive and take possession of the keys. A refundable deposit equal to the entire rental amount is paid in cash upon arrival.
> 6 rue du Sentier, 2e
TEL: 01 42 963 146
www.parisattitude.com

Lodgis.com is truly a site for the jet-setters. Short- and long-term rentals are on offer for Paris, London, New York, Marrakech and the French Riviera. Paris apartment listings are presented with numerous photos and detailed descriptions including prices, availability and apartment amenities. The Web site is easy to use with settings for maximum budget and area. Fees are based on the length of the rental which is included in the price listed on the site. Typically the fee will be 25% of the total rental price.
> 47 rue de Paradis, 10e
6 rue Le Goff, 5e
TEL: (33) 1 70 39 11 11
www.lodgis.com

EATS

Forget the nutrition pyramid—it's a vacation! Kids' five favorite food groups: French fries, chocolate milk, burgers, ketchup and grilled cheese. It's kid-approved. We've carefully selected great lunch options near popular sights because, who are you kidding, you'll be dialing "0" for room service (clearly the most sensible option after a long day of sight-seeing) at dinner time. Bon appetit!

The choices listed below are divided by neighborhood/landmark, then by category, such as restaurant, bistro, café, restaurant chain, *crêperie,* tea salon, ice cream parlor and the occasional wine bar. If you do not see a desired landmark listing, then you may want to choose another place to visit around mealtime—here you'll find the most convenient, timeless, classic and budget-friendly meals Paris has to offer.

Before you head off, here are some tips to make your dinner, lunch, or tea more enjoyable: Most Parisians tend to have lunch between 1 p.m. and 2 p.m.; dinner usually starts around 8 p.m. or 8:30 p.m. for adults. Try to make reservations in advance, especially on Thursday, Friday and Saturday nights. Many restaurants, much like the rest of Paris, are closed on Sundays.

NEAR THE *JARDIN DU LUXEMBOURG*

Cafés abound in the area, as do bakeries and *crêperies* and *épiceries* (gourlet-shop)-restaurants.

Bakeries

Looking for the best buttery croissants?
Try **Gerard Mulot,** a place known as the "breakfast of senators" because of the nearby Senate, located in the *Palais du Luxembourg.*
> 7 rue de Seine, 6ᵉ
Mᴇ́ᴛʀᴏ: Oᴅᴇᴏɴ
Tᴇʟ: 01 43 268 577
Tɪᴍɪɴɢs: Cʟᴏsᴇᴅ Wᴇᴅɴᴇsᴅᴀʏ

Patisserie Dalloyau: These folks are known as the Picassos of Patisserie and have over 200 years of history to prove it. The in-house tearoom provides a great temptation to sit and rest. Well-heeled grandmothers and mothers bring their offspring here en route for a play date in the nearby *Jardin du Luxembourg.*
> 2 place Edmond-Rostand, 6ᵉ
Tel: 01 43 293 110

For sit-down *crêpes*, try **Crêperie des Arts.** There's usually a line, probably because children can do a taste test before making a selection.
> 27 rue Saint-André-des-Arts, 6ᵉ
Tel: 01 43 261 568

Da Rosa Epicerie-Cantine offers enviable tapas including lardo, strips of po⸍ ⸍ ⸍ cured with sea salt and herbs by a Michelin chef. Sharing communal tables is part of the experience. The kiddies may be more inclined to sample if they see their fellow diners diving into the food with gusto. You can feast on foie gras, the most delectable Spanish ham you have ever tasted, rich chocolates, fabulous cheeses, a few hot dishes, and wines, too. Be sure the buy the big bag of chocolate-coated Sauternes-soaked raisins on your way out.
> 62 rue de Seine, near the *rue de Buci* market, 6e
Mᴇ́ᴛʀᴏ: Oᴅᴇᴏɴ
Tᴇʟ: 01 40 510 009
Hᴏᴜʀs: 10 A.M. TO 10 P.M.

Ice cream

Amorino, 4 rue Vavin, 6ᵉ

COST: A SMALL CONE COSTS €3

AT THE EIFFEL TOWER

Restaurant: The famous—and famously expensive—*Le Jules Verne* restaurant on the second platform has its own private elevator in the south pillar; reservations are mandatory for both lunch and dinner. It's quite popular, so book at least a month in advance. Children are welcome, but there's no kid's menu

> Eiffel Tower, 2ⁿᵈ platform

TEL: 01 45 556 144

Bistro: There are more humble eateries, including *Altitude 95* on the first platform, and a snack bar, so you won't go hungry 95 meters up from sea level. But if eating up high isn't your idea of a good time, trek back down and check out the cafés within easier reach of the average budget.

> Eiffel tower, 1ˢᵗ platform

TEL: 01 45 552 004

Restaurant Chain

Bistro Romain

6 place Victor Hugo, 16ᵉ

TEL: 01 45 006 503 (SEE **FAMILY FRIENDLY RESTAURANT CHAINS** FOR MORE LOCATIONS).

NEAR THE *MUSÉE PICASSO*

Brasserie: *Le Petit Bofinger:* This brasserie is located across the street from its famous and world-renowned big brother, the *belle époque* **Bofinger**, founded in 1864. *Le Petit Bofinger* is the preferred choice for most families. Why? The children's menu is €7 and the food is delicious. If the fame and glory of Bofinger itself lures you in—it is like a grand, *Art Nouveau* movie set, right down to the sparking glass roof and wrought-iron staircase. The *Bofinger* offers a children's menu for €12.50. Best behavior (for the kids, not you) is advisable and waiters are not the friendliest in town. There is a nice view of the *Place de la Bastille* from the outside tables, and it is only a 10-minute walk from the *Musée Picasso.*

> 6 rue de la Bastille, 4ᶜ, (Note: this restaurant location is one of four in town)

TEL: 01 42 720 523

www.bofingerparis.com

IN THE *JARDIN D'ACCLIMATATION*

Restaurant: Twice a week, an incredible and substantial family-style buffet is served in the *Pavilion des Oiseaux au Jardin d'Acclimation.* It can't get much easier and child-friendly than to plan your day around this great and casual ambience of child-dedicated fun. **Buffet times:** Wednesdays at noon and Sundays at 1p.m. Reservations highly recommended. In addition to the buffet, there are magicians, face painting and clowns for entertainment.

On Wednesdays, children can attend a theater workshop at 1 p.m. After the Sunday buffet, there is a percussion workshop.
> Inside the Jardin d'Acclimation, Bois de Boulogne, 16ᵉ
Tel: 01 45 021 161
Price for children's buffet: €23.60; under 4 years old: €6.90. The price also includes workshop.

NEAR THE *JARDIN DES TUILERIES*

Quick and Easy Food: Louvre Food Court is conveniently located in the *Carrousel du Louvre* Shopping Center. Even the pickiest gourmand will find something to like at the food court. Enter from underground or the *rue de Rivoli* entrance. Restrooms available under the stairs/next to the escalators on the *rue de Rivoli* side.

Tea Salon: *Salon du Thé Angelina* serves a world-famous, very rich, *Le Chocolat Africain* (hot chocolate) and pastries. This is a place where much of the fashion world snacks and lunches between runway shows. The spacious restrooms upstairs have no changing table, but there is space to spread out on the floor, if you bring your own changing mat.
> Across from the *Tuileries* Gardens, 226, rue de Rivoli, 1ᵉ

NEAR THE *MUSÉE DE LA POUPÉE*

Tea Salon: After your tour, sit down for a *"goûter"* or snack at *Mariage Frères,* the elegant, colonial tea house and museum in the Marais, about a 10-15 minute walk away. There are a number of *Mariage Frères* around Paris, but this is the original, established in 1854. *Mariage Frères* will transport you into an appealing and pleasurable world. The aroma of over 300 varieties of teas from over 20 countries will invade your senses, while the sounds of classical music and the pleasant interior will all add to your understanding of why this is one of France's oldest and most respected tea houses. It is best to come for breakfast or tea; the food itself is a bit overpriced and not as spectacular as the teas. Small, handsome restrooms on ground level. Brunch served on weekends.
> 30-32 rue du Bourg-Tibourg, 4ᵉ
Tel: 01 42 72 28 11
Hours: Daily 10:30 a.m. to 7:30 p.m.
Credit Cards accepted.
www.mariagefreres.fr
Also see Centre Pompidou listing for nearby eats.

NEAR THE *OPÉRA GARNIER*

Café: There are only a handful of cafés in the world as grand as the *Café de la Paix,* partly due to the fact that this place was designed by the same Garnier who was responsible for the neighboring *Opéra Garnier.* This is a place to see and be seen, from early morning to late at night. For families,

afternoon tea is the best time to sit and enjoy the incredible view of the *Opéra Garnier*. Not for the light-of-wallet—it is expensive. Well-equipped restrooms with changing table upstairs.
> 12 blvd des Capucines, 9^e
Tel: 01 40 073 010

NEAR THE CATACOMBS
Restaurants: *Hippopotamus* serves up "steak-frites" and other meat and potato dishes and is always reliable and child-friendly. (See Family-friendly restaurant chains for more locations).
> Alésia, 80 av Général Leclerc, 14^e
Korean Barbecue is a traditional Korean barbecue restaurant. Kids can pile up their plates with a variety of meats, veggies and sauces. A chef will then assist with the grilling on the grill located in the middle of the table. Pile the goodies high, because the food tends to shrink to the size of miniature shrimps.
> 39 rue du Montparnasse 14^e
Tel: 01 43 276 953

IN THE *PRINTEMPS* DEPARTMENT STORE
Brasserie: Don't shop until you drop; just shop until you're hungry. Head to *Brasserie Flo,* located on the top floor of the *Printemps* department store. Take a seat and order lunch under the famous *Art Nouveau* dome, consisting of 3,185 multicolored glass sections and floral motifs. It's a national treasure and breathtakingly

beautiful. Try to start lunch early, as it tends to get crowded.
> Printemps department store, 6th floor
Tel: 01 42 825 884

NEAR THE *LE VILLAGE JOUÉCLUB*
Restaurant chain: *Léon de Bruxelles* offers up a casual atmosphere, and is well known to turn the fussiest eaters into *moules-frites* (steamed mussels with French fries) lovers. The generous children's menu offers all the staples: burgers, French fries and chicken.
> 30 blvd Italiens, 9^e
(See Family-friendly restaurant chains for more locations).
Tel: 01 55 612 408
www.leon-de-bruxelles.fr

Brasserie: Down the road, at the corner of *rue Quatre-Septembre* and *rue de Richelieu,* the more intimate neighborhood café *L'Ami Georges* is great for *frites* and café fare, and offers a real non-smoking area. It caters to kids and parents alike. Basic restroom downstairs.
> 5 rue du Quatre-Septembre, 2^e
Tel: 01 42 974 888

NEAR THE *MUSÉE D'ORSAY*
Café: *Le Café Marly* is located across from the *Louvre,* and is only recommended if the weather permits you to enjoy the outside terrace. Kids can run around I.M. Pei's glass pyramid while parents

sip lattes or a well-deserved glass of wine. The place is not cheap: dinner for a family of four can cost €200, not including drinks. Instead, try stopping by in the late afternoon for coffee or a glass of wine. This place could be a contender as one of the top five places in the world to enjoy an outstanding view of Paris.

> 93 rue de Rivoli, 1ᵉ

Tᴇʟ: 01 49 260 660

AT/NEAR THE *CENTRE POMPIDOU*

Restaurants

On the 6ᵗʰ floor of the *Centre Pompidou, Georges* is a trendy and expensive place to eat. There is a big open terrace offering a spectacular view of Paris. Don't want to spend a fortune on lunch or dinner? Try late afternoon snacks on the outside terrace. Of course, sunset is the best time to visit.

> *Centre Pompidou*, 6ᵗʰ Floor

01 44 784 799

Le Trumilou is a lively and rather capacious dining area filled with Parisian families, especially on weekends. According to the New York Times, the food here is what you dream about eating, if only you had a French mother-in-law! Reasonably-priced, it also offers friendly service, especially with children in tow. A visit here will give you that "Yes, I'm in Paris" feeling.

> 84 quai de l'Hôtel de Ville, 4ᵉ

Tᴇʟ: 01 42 776 398

The Art Deco interior of *Vaudeville,* including loads of mirrors and marble, is just about always packed with Parisians and tourists alike. At times it can be noisy, but still fun for the kids, especially thanks to the friendly staff. If it does get too overwhelming, a table on the sidewalk terrace is another option. Service is fast, and it's been bustling and dependable since the doors opened in 1925.

> 29 rue Vivienne, 2ᵉ

Tᴇʟ: 01 40 200 462

www.vaudeville.com

Cafés: *Café Mezzanine* (1ˢᵗ floor) and the *Kiosque* (2ⁿᵈ floor) in the *Centre Pompidou* offer fast food alternatives.

24-hour bistro

Pied de Cochon is famous for its onion soup. This classic and timeless bistro is also a bit touristy. Open 24 hours a day, 365 days a year.

> 6 rue Coquillières, 1ᵉ

Tᴇʟ: 01 40 137 700

Hᴏᴜʀs: Dᴀɪʟʏ, 24 ʜᴏᴜʀs

www.pieddecochon.com

Outdoor courtyard

Le Studio is a Tex-Mex place that offers a simple outdoor courtyard where kids can run around so parents don't have to. Most children can be easily entertained by watching the various dance classes that are held across the courtyard.

> 41 rue du Temple, 4ᵉ

Tel: 01 42 741 038
http://the-studio.fr
(Also see Musée de la Poupée listing
for nearby eats).

NEAR THE *MUSÉE NATIONAL D'HISTOIRE NATURELLE*

Restaurant: *Polidor* is a classic, affordable Parisian bistro, considered to be one of the oldest in Paris. The restaurant's name dates back to the early 1900s, when it specialized in crème desserts. However, its history even goes back further, to 1845. Known by generations as a neighborhood eatery offering inexpensive, family-style cooking served at long tables with checkered cloth-covered tables, it's perfect for ... families. A two-course meal costs just €10. Of special interest to kids: this place still has old-style squatting toilets—there are hardly any left in town. Be sure to investigate the paintings on the walls, all by local artists.
> 41 rue Monsieur-le-Prince, 6ᵉ
Tel: 01 43 269 534
www.restaurantpolidor.info

NEAR THE *ARC DE TRIOMPHE*

Pomze, another épicerie, is all about apples and what can be done with them. There's Granny Smith jam, recipes made with Juliets and *Calvados* and an unlimited number of ciders. A great lunch option.

109 blvd Haussmann, 8e
Tel: 01 42 656 583

Take away: *Lina's Sandwiches* is a chain restaurant located throughout Paris. They serve US-style (meaning big) sandwiches and salads.
> 8 rue Marbeuf, 8ᵉ
Tel: 01 47 239 233

NEAR *LE BON MARCHÉ* DEPARTMENT STORE

Brasserie: In the *Hotel Lutétia,* there is the Brasserie Lutétia. This place offers a delightfully airy space with good food—and a children's menu. Downstairs restroom offers a changing table.
> 45 blvd Raspail, 6ᵉ
Tel: 01 49 544 676
www.lutetia-paris.com

Gourmet grocery store: The *Grande Epicerie* grocery store is a gourmet food-lover's delight and it's just next door to the *Le Bon Marché* department store. The ideal place to find picnic fare or take-away snacks, it's not exactly cheap, but there's a wide selection of food that the kids will enjoy
> 24 rue de Sèvres, 7ᵉ
Tel: 01 44 398 000
Hours: 9:30 a.m. to 7 p.m., Mon to Wed; 10 a.m. to 9 p.m. Thurs; 9:30 a.m. to 8 p.m. Sat
www.bonmarche.fr

NEAR THE *QUAI BRANLY*

Café: *L'Ancien Trocadero* is a sidewalk café that offers a good view of the *Palais du Chaillot*, but the real attraction here is the reasonable prices for salads and burgers.

> 2 place du Trocadero, 16ᵉ
Tᴇʟ: 01 47 274 249
Cʜɪʟᴅʀᴇɴ's ᴍᴇɴᴜ €11.40 (ɪɴᴄʟᴜᴅɪɴɢ ɪᴄᴇ ᴄʀᴇᴀᴍ)

NEAR THE *HOTEL DES INVALIDES* AND *MUSÉE RODIN*

Bistro: *Bistro Thoumieux* is a large, quintessentially Parisian bistro. It is an ideal place for Sunday brunch, among a clientele consisting mostly of young city dwellers and local families. With the bustling waiters in their white aprons and the red-velour banquettes, it feels like nothing has changed here over the three generations that is has been owned and operated by the same family. Good value for money, with a set menu starting at €13.

> 79 rue St-Dominique, 7ᵉ
Tᴇʟ: 01 47 054 975
www.thoumieux.com

NEAR THE *CATHEDRAL NOTRE-DAME DE PARIS*

Ice cream: *Berthillon* is the most famous and popular place in Paris to buy ice cream, it has been supplying locals and visitors since 1954. *Berthillon* is known for its quality and the wide variety of flavors available—there are at least five different varieties of chocolate

ice cream. It is 100% kid-approved.

> 31 rue Saint-Louis-en-l'Ile, 4ᵉ
Tᴇʟ: 01 43 543 161
Hᴏᴜʀs: 10 ᴀ.ᴍ. ᴛᴏ 8 ᴘ.ᴍ. Cʟᴏsᴇᴅ Mᴏɴ, Tᴜᴇs, ᴀɴᴅ ᴍɪᴅ-Jᴜʟʏ ᴛᴏ ᴛʜᴇ ʙᴇɢɪɴɴɪɴɢ ᴏғ Sᴇᴘᴛ. Cʀᴇᴅɪᴛ ᴄᴀʀᴅs ᴀᴄᴄᴇᴘᴛᴇᴅ.

NEAR THE *PLACE DES INVALIDES*

Croissants/Pain au chocolat:
Patisserie Millet Croissants aren't just for breakfast anymore, at least not in France. Children here stop by their local pastry shop after school to score their all-time favorite snack which is *pain au chocolat*. This treat is just like a croissant, but with a stick or two of bittersweet chocolate in the middle. It is then baked until the chocolate oozes out of the sides. Yummmmm. *Patisserie Millet* turns out more than 500 croissants, six days a week—that's how good they are.

> 103 rue St. Dominique, 7ᵉ
Tᴇʟ: 01 45 514 980
Hᴏᴜʀs: Tᴜᴇs ᴛᴏ Sᴀᴛ 9 ᴀ.ᴍ. ᴛᴏ 7ᴘ.ᴍ.; Sᴜɴ 8 ᴀ.ᴍ. ᴛᴏ 1 ᴘ.ᴍ. Cʟᴏsᴇᴅ Mᴏɴ.

MUSÉE DE QUAI BRANLY

Cafés: The *Musée de Quai Branly* cafe—*Café Branly* is adjacent to the museum and serves small portions of salads, pastas and quiches. It is tempting to stop en route and afterwards. Some tables offer a nice view of the Eiffel Tower. *Les Ombres*, the upstairs semi-formal dining restaurant offers excellent rofftop views of the Eiffel tower with price tag to match.

> *Café Branly & Les Ombres,*
27 quai Branly, 7^e
Tel: 01 47 536 800

Lenôtre shops are a good bet for croissants, too. There are over 10 shops located throughout Paris, with the favorite listed below.
> Lenôtre, 3-5 rue du Havre, 9^e
Tel: 01 45 222 259

WORTH A DETOUR
These locations are great places to get food, even if you have to make a special trip.

Cafés
Cafe de Flore is located just a few steps from **Les Deux Magots** (see below), these two cafes will be forever known as arch rivals. Here at the *Café de Flore,* the best action tends to take place downstairs, including at the sidewalk tables. It's a place where famous celebs and many regulars mix and mingle, and is a great location for people watching, even with kids. Jean Paul Sartre and Simone de Beauvoir used to rendezvous here, and the folks here claim they can show you the very table where Sartre and de Beauvoir used to sit. Kids can color on the house placemats and take them home as souvenirs. On Mondays, as well as the first Wednesday of every month, there are readings and philosophy discussions in English, at 8 p.m.
> 172 blvd Saint-Germain, 6^e
Tel: 01 45 485 526
Hours: 7:30 a.m. to 1:30 p.m., a.m. daily

Credit cards accepted

Les Deux Magots offers one of the most appealing terraces on *Saint-Germain-des-Près*, as well as an exceptional view of the church of *Saint-Germain-des-Près*. The kids can color on the house placemats here, too, for even more souvenirs. Be sure to sit under the famous wooden statues of the two Chinese maggots (dignitaries) that decorate one of the pillars. Noteworthy tidbit: the church of *Saint-Germain-des-Prés*, right across the street, is the oldest church in Paris.
> 170 blvd St-Germain, 6^e
Tel: 01 45 485 525
Hours: 7:30 a.m. to 2 a.m. daily
Credit cards accepted

Pastry shop: For over 20 years, *Daniel Walter* has created desserts, pastries, tartelettes, and parfaits. This shop, known as Walter, could easily be classified as a historic landmark for any Parisian. It is also highly recommended by the Louis Vuitton-carrying, artistic, jet-setting crowd.
> *Walter,* 7 rue Brézin, 14^e
Tel: 01 45 394 602
Hours: 8 a.m. to 7:45 p.m.; closed Mon
Credit cards accepted

Tea salons
Fauchon is perhaps the most famous luxury grocery store/deli in Paris, if not the whole of France. Around since 1886, many consider

it to be one of the best places in Paris for croissants, and it is also known for supplying exotic fruit that can't be found anywhere else in Paris—at anytime of the year. It is an ideal place to stop and build a gourmet picnic. The gift packaging alone is worth a visit, making it ideal for souvenirs and gifts to take back home to the in-laws.

> 26-30 place de la Madeleine, 8ᵉ

Tel: 01 47 42 60 11

Hours: 9:30 a.m. to 7 p.m. Mon to Sat; closed on Sun and public holidays

www.fauchon.fr

Ladurée is a quintessential French tea salon and is among the best Paris has to offer. Conveniently located halfway down the *Avenue des Champs-Elysées,* it is a perfect rest stop between shopping sprees. Established in 1862, it still offers up its famous macaroons: two biscuits sandwiched together with a layer of fluffy cream. These mouth-watering treats were invented in the early 20th century, and come in every possible color and flavor. Try the citron vert-basilic (lime and basil) or the old favorite chocolat noir (dark chocolate). The décor is quite upscale: better not to visit while wearing jeans or shorts.

> 75 av des Champs-Elysées, 8ᵉ

Métro: Georges V

> 16 rue Royale, 8ᵉ

Tel: 01 40 750 8 75/01 42 602 179

Hours: 8:30 a.m. to 7 p.m. Mon to Sat; 10 a.m. to 7 p.m. Sun

American/English grocery stores

You came all the way to Paris, and shopping for American food is probably the last thing on your mind. But just in case you find yourself in need of familiar, reliable, American diapers, peanut butter, macaroni and cheese, or Oreos—it is all here. If, heaven forbid, your little ones start exhibiting flu symptoms, and you are in dire need of a can of Campbell's soup or Children's Tylenol, this is the place to get it. Aside from some good old, American, can't-live-without-it favorites, this place serves up awesome Louisiana Cajun- and Creole-based dishes that are sure to get you wondering where you are—Paris or Louisiana.

> **Thanksgiving**

20 Rue Saint-Paul, 4e

Métro: St. Paul

Tel: 01 42 776 828

Hours: Open for lunch and dinner Wed to Sat; brunch on Sat and Sun; Closed Sun evening, Mon and Tue; first two weeks of Aug.; last week of Dec.

www.thanksgiving.paris.com

> **The Real McCoy**

194 Rue de Grenelle, 7e

Metro: École Militaire

Tel: 01 45 569 882

Hours: Open 7 days a week, 10 A.M. to 8 P.M.

> **Scrumptious** (Near *Musée de l'Eventail*)

68 Quai Jemmapes, 10e

Métro: Strasbourg-St.-Denis

Bus: 38, 39, 47

Hours: Wed to Sun 8 A.M. to 10 P.M.

FAMILY-FRIENDLY RESTAURANT CHAINS (WHEN YOU NEED A RELIABLE FAVORITE)

Hippopotamus: The *Hippopotamus* chain is the most popular, and a true favorite among Parisian families. It even has a nickname: Hippo, as it's generally known throughout Paris. The staff is friendly and every child receives a gift bag with balloons, coloring books, games and puzzles. The menu consists of burgers, steaks, ribs and baked potatoes. If anyone in the family has a sweet tooth, there are lots of desserts. The ice cream sundaes are billed as the all-time favorite. Children menu €7.50. Several locations throughout the city.
Hippopotamus (favorite locations)
> 1 blvd Beaumarchais, 4e
Tel: 01 44 619 040
> 9 rue Lagrange, 5e
Tel: 01 43 541 399
> 29 rue Berger, 1e
Tel: 01 45 080 029
> 81 blvd des Capucines, 2e
Tel: 01 47 427 570
>42 av des Champs-Elysées, 8e
Tel: 01 45 634 084
www.hippopotamus.fr (for other locations)

Bistro Romain: A place where the kid's menu includes lasagna, burgers and piles of fries. It also offers up ice cream and chocolate mousse and it's all you can eat. (Most popular locations)

> 26 av des Champs-Elysées, 8e
Tel: 01 53 751 784
> 122 av des Champs-Elysées, 8e
Tel: 01 53 751 784
> 6 place Victor Hugo, 16e
Tel: 01 45 006 503
> 222 rue de la Convention
Tel: 01 53 686 451
www.bistroromain.fr/ (for other locations)

Chez Clement: The copper pots and seasonal décor is the signature style here, along with the most generous food portions—for both adults and children—in all of Paris. The place has great, casual ambience, and offers reasonable rates. A three-course lunch for an adult runs €17.50, while the children's fare is an amazing €7.80 euro for lunch or dinner. Service is nonstop, too, so you can come when it suits you. The *Champs-Elysées* location offers view of the *Arc de Triomphe*.
> 123 av des Champs-Elysées
Tel: 01 40 738 700
www.chezclement.com (for other locations)

Léon de Bruxelles: This Belgian chain is famous as the place for mussels and fries; it also offers a wide variety of brasserie-type food. The children's menu is incredibly reasonable.
> 8 place de la Republic
Tel: 01 43 382 519
www.leon-de bruxelles.fr (for other locations)

Pizza hut: Desperate and in need of delivery? The always reliable and dependable Pizza Hut is just a phone call away. Well, that's "pizza hoot" in French. This may come as a bit of a shock to some Francophiles out there, but French moms need an occasional break from the kitchen, too. (Even Domino's gets in on the act!). Pizza Hut has several locations throughout Paris; ask your hotel for the nearest one.
> 22 bis rue Jean Nicot, 7ᵉ
TEL: 08 25 030 030
www.pizzahut.fr

Joe Allen's: This chain offers a good, traditional American-style brunch. The old jukebox brings an atmosphere of fun and flare to the place. Locations in New York, London and Miami Beach, as well.
> 30 rue Pierre Lescot, 1ᵉ
TEL: 01 42 367 013
www.joeallenrestaurant.com
(for other locations)

Quick Hamburger Restaurant: It's the McDonald's of Europe with the typical fast-food joint fare. Most, if not all, have mini indoor playgrounds.
Healthy fast-food chain.

Lina's Sandwiches: There are several of these shops throughout Paris. They all serve USA-style sandwiches and salads.
> 116 av Kleber, 16ᵉ (small outlet)
Tel: 01 47 272 828
> 7 av de l'Opéra, 1ᵉ
TEL: 01 47 033 029

Organic food chain

Le Pain Quotidien: French for "Daily Bread," serves not only superb bread, such as pain ancienne, baguettes, peasant bread and rye but delicious, mouthwatering sandwiches and salads, as well. All locations in Paris, as well as several U.S. locations. There are over 60 locations throughout the world which carry the signature decor of a rustic countryside charm where guests share in a communal meal on long wooden tables. It is a bit more on the expensive side.
> 18 pl. du Marché-Saint-Honoré, 1ᵉ
TEL: 01 42 963 170
> 33 rue Vivienne, 2ᵉ
TEL: 01 42 367 602
> 2 rue des Petits Carreaux, 2ᵉ
TEL: 01 42 211 450
> 18-20 rue des Archives, 4ᵉ
TEL: 01 44 540 307
> 38 rue Mouffetard, 5ᵉ
TEL: 01 55 439 199
www.lepainquotidien.com

SHOPPING

Oh-la-la, c'est tres chic ! Toy-riffic and trendy—
from groovy gadgets to snazzy clothing for your
mini travel companion and more.

It goes without saying that children's clothing in Paris is expensive; but finding amazing and affordable boutiques and shops in little Madeleine's hometown is surprisingly easy. Here is a condensed list of our top picks.

TOYS

Au Nain Bleu is the most luxurious and the largest toy store in Paris. This place has been a Parisian favorite since its doors opened in 1836. It's the FAO Schwartz of Paris, offering three floors filled with the kind of toys that both grown-ups and children would want to have. It's the largest, fanciest and certainly the oldest toy store in Paris. The toys are expensive, but the first floor offers a few more reasonable finds. Plus, this is the place to find those fantastic wooden sailboats that Parisian children use in the fountains in the *Luxembourg* or *Tuilleries*.

> 406-410 rue St. Honoré, 8^e
Tel: 01 42 603 901
Hours: 10 a.m. to 6:30 p.m. Mon to Sat
www.au-nain-bleu.fr

La Grande Récré is located in the front of *Cité des Sciences et de l'Industrie (Cité des Enfants)*. It offers a cheaper alternative for gifts to take home.

> *Cité des Sciences et de l'Industrie (Cité des Enfants)*
32 av Corentin Cariou, 19^e
Tel: 01 46 070 037
Hours: 10 a.m. to 19 p.m. Mon to Sat
www.la-grande-recre.com

Pain d'Epices is a marvelous shop that offers everything a little girl could want for her dollhouse. It is full of treasures such as adorable miniature baguettes and French shopping baskets, along with tiny sweets jars, plants, cans, bottles ... you name it. There is everything a girl ever dreamed of to give Dolly's home-sweet-home a little French flair.

> 29 passage Jouffroy, 9^e
Tel: 01 47 70 08 68
Hours: 12:30 p.m. to 7 p.m. Mon; 10 a.m. to 7 p.m. Tue to Sat; until 9 p.m. Thu
www.paindepices.fr

CLOTHES

Minika sells a few well-known labels at discount prices and they also offer children's haircuts, a kid's video show and desks with crayons to keep the whippersnappers entertained.
> 38 place Vendôme, 1^e

Just about every savvy and stylish Parisian mother will confess that **Rue Vavin, 6^e** is one of her local favorite shopping areas for their children. Located only yards away from the **Jardin du Luxembourg,** this quarter-mile-long street is jam-packed with children's clothing boutiques and other goodies including: **Du Pariel au Même, Catimini, Froment-LeRoyer** (children's shoes), **Jacadi, Neck and Neck, Marie Papier** and **Petit Bateau,** to name a few favorites. This is a one-stop shopping area at its best. There is also a **FNAC Junior**—a French favorite for books and educational toys—at the top of the street.

Du Pariel au Même
> 17 rue Vavin, 6ᵉ
Tᴇʟ: 01 43 541 234

Catimini
> 10 rue Vavin, 6ᵉ
Tᴇʟ: 01 44 410 233

Froment-LeRoyer
> 7 rue Vavin, 6ᵉ
Tᴇʟ: 01 43 543 315

Jacadi
> 26 rue Vavin, 6ᵉ
Tᴇʟ: 01 40 519 553

Neck and Neck
> 3 rue Vavin, 6ᵉ
Tᴇʟ: 01 46 334 976

Marie Papier
> 26 rue Vavin, 6ᵉ
Tᴇʟ: 01 43 264 644

Petit Bateau
> 26 rue Vavin, 6ᵉ
Tᴇʟ: 01 43 264 644

FNAC Junior
> 19 rue Vavin, 6ᵉ
Tᴇʟ: 08 92 350 666

Repetto is a charming 50-year-old boutique which was started by a ballerina. The owner created her own ballet shoes, and became a fashion favorite almost overnight for such 1960s film stars as *Brigitte Bardot* and co. Now the company offers a *prêt-a-porter* (ready-to-wear) line for children ages 2-12. It's sure to be a prima ballerina favorite for any gal, and it keeps the rest of Paris on its toes. Adorable petticoat skirts and *cache-coeur* wraps are pirouetting right out the door.
> 22 rue de la Paix, 2ᵉ
Tᴇʟ: 01 44 718 312

Agnes B Enfant helps little divas get that pulled-together Parisian schoolgirl look. The clothing is a bit expensive. Offering sizes from baby to age 14. A fashionable Parisian name, and you'll pay the prices to prove it.
> 2 rue du Jour, 1^e
Tel: 01 45 085 656

Bonpoint offers classic and tailored clothes at reasonable prices. With over 15 locations throughout Paris, the Bonpoint flagship store, located in a lovely 17th century building, offers a tearoom and private garden for customers. It's worth a visit, especially since the Luxembourg Gardens are only a few minutes away. There is a discount shop selling the previous seasons clothing at **Bonpoint Fin de Series.**
> **Bonpoint**, 6 rue de Tournon, 6^e
Tel: 01 40 519 820
www.bonpoint.fr
> **Bonpoint Fin de Series**
42 rue de l'Université, 7^e
Tel: 01 40 201 055

Tout Compte Fait offers chic and affordable French basics for children, up to size 12. There are over 17 locations throughout Paris.
> 128 Faubourg St. Antoine, 12^e
Tel: 01 43 469 432
> 31 rue Saint-Placide, 6^e
Tel: 01 42 224 564
> 170 rue du Temple, 3^e
Tel: 01 40 27 00 42
www.toutcomptefait.com (for other locations)

If you can only make one stop for children's clothing, make it **Du Pareil au Même.** It is cheap chic at its best. If you ever wonder how Parisian children always look so pulled-together, it's because their moms shop here. It has been around for two decades and covers babies to pre-teens. There are over 27 locations throughout Paris.
> 120-22 rue du Faubourg St. Antoine, 12^e
Tel: 01 43 446 746
www.dpam.com

Sergent Major stocks affordable and good-quality clothing for children up to 14 years old. There are several locations throughout Paris, and it's well known for quality, très mignons (very cute) boys' clothes.
> 109 av Victor Hugo, 16^e
Tel: 01 53 651 218
www.sergent-major.com (for other locations)

Paul and Joe at the end of Avenue Montaigne is a light and airy boutique which specializes in hip women's clothing. Named after the designer's son, the style quotient of the cute, though small selection of children's clothing is definitely retro and certainly funky.
> 2 avenue Montaigne, 8e
Tel: 01 40 280 334
Hours: 10 A.M. TO 7 P.M. DAILY; CLOSED ON SUN
www.paulandjoe.com for other locations

OUTLET/BARGAIN SHOPPING

Known as "outlet street", *Rue d'Alesia* includes many discount shops offering ready-to-wear collections. Among the worthwhile finds for children is the **Cacharel Stock Shop.**

> *Du Pareil au Même*
114 rue d'Alesia
TEL: 01 45 425 504

Tati is truly a legendary bargain hunter's paradise for discount goods. The secret is to mix-and-match, so a scarf might be the only item you will find here on one visit, while next time you might buy a matching pair of pants. The children's clothes are a bargain, though not always the highest quality. Hunting is definitely part of the game and there are some real gems to be found. If you are in the neighborhood and have time it's worth taking a peek. **Beware:** Saturday is the busiest day of the week.

> 4 blvd de Rochehouart, 18ᵉ
TEL: 01 55 295 250
HOURS: 10 A.M. TO 7 P.M. MON TO SAT
> Centre Commercial Italie 2
TEL: 01 53 809 770
> 76 av de Clichy, 17ᵉ
TEL: 01 58 22 2 890
www.tati.fr (for other locations)

SPORTS/CASUAL WEAR

Citadium is a hip and cool place that offers the latest and most stylish active sportswear to be found in Paris. It is owned and operated by the Au Printemps department store folks. On Saturday afternoons, DJs spin music.

> 50-56 rue Caumartine, 9ᵉ
TEL: 01 55 317 400
www.citadium.fr

Okaidi is the French version of a Gap store for children. With over 10 locations in Paris, and several more located all over France and Belgium, this French chain is very popular and quite hip. The two-story flagship store near the Bastille has a good selection of the basics.

> 32 rue Charles-Baudelaire, 12ᵉ
TEL: 01 53 338 886
www.okaidi.com (for other locations)

BOUTIQUES

Calesta Kidstore houses two stories filled with the most indulgent of children's items to be found. Fashion-obsessed Parisian parents confess that this store is a favorite. Suitable for children up to 10 years of age.

> 23 rue Debelleyme, 3ᵉ
TEL: 01 42 721 559

Le Marchand d'Etoiles is a quaint little boutique run by an American-turned-Parisian, offering a line of sleepwear for newborns and young children, plus baby cribs, pillows and sheets sets, stuffed animals, books and more. The store is located one block away from the world-famous department store, *Le Bon Marche*. Storybook readings are offered in English and French monthly.

> 3 rue Chomel, 7^e

TᴇL: 01 42 844 202

Blink and you will miss it, Talc, is a tiny boutique located near *Le Marchand d'Etoiles*. Well-made children's clothing in timeless styles can be found here.

>60 rue de Saintonge, 3^e

TᴇL: 01 42 775 263

>65 rue de Turene, 4^e

Tel: 01 42 716 812

SOME MORE OF OUR FAVORITES

All the stores listed here are relatively expensive, but offer traditional clothing styles. All have several locations; we have listed the most centrally located.

Catimini: Over seven locations throughout Paris.

> 114 av des Champs-Elysées, 8^e

TᴇL: 01 53 762 151

www.catimini.com (for other locations)

Natalys: Offering more than just children's clothing, high quality nursery and baby equipment can also be found here. Over seven locations throughout Paris.

> 92 av des Champs-Elysées, 8^e

TᴇL: 01 43 591 765

www.natalys.fr (for other locations)

Tartine et Chocolat: Over four locations throughout Paris.

> 266 blvd St. Germain, 7^e

TᴇL: 01 45 561 045

www.tartine-et-chocolat.fr

Petit Bateau: Perfect and practical T-shirts and pajamas for children of all ages. Several locations throughout Paris.

> 116 av des Champs-Elysées, 8^e

TᴇL: 01 40 740 203

www.petitbateau.fr

DEPARTMENT STORES

Galeries Lafayette: This historic and world-renowned department store, in its 10-story art-nouveau building with stained glass dome, is a shopping landmark for any visitor. It offers loads of designer and brand-name items in clothing and much, much more.

> 40 blvd Haussman, 9^e

TᴇL: 01 42 823 456

Hᴏᴜʀs: 9:30 ᴀ.ᴍ. ᴛᴏ 6:45 ᴘ.ᴍ. Mᴏɴ ᴛᴏ Sᴀᴛ; 9 ᴘ.ᴍ. ᴏɴ Tʜᴜ

www.lafayettegalleries.com (for other locations)

BHV (Bazar de l'Hotel de Ville) is one of the oldest department stores in Paris. Open since 1852, over its eight levels, you'll find everything you expect from a major French department store clothing, home decor, linens, furniture, appliances, and hardware. *BHV*'s hardware department is renowned as a paradise for DIYers. This is

also one of the least expensive department stores in Paris and is usually packed.
> 52 64 rue de Rivoli, 4ᵉ
TEL: 01 42 749 000
www.bhv.fr

Au Printemps carries everything from children's books to concert hall tickets and other fabulous finds. It is located just minutes from the *Opera Garnier. Au Printemps* offers a personal shopping service, including both fashion and decorating advice; hotel and worldwide deliveries; and a check-room for strollers and purchases. There are also two hair salons, two beauty institutes for women, a body care institute for men, and a ticket office for shows, museums and concerts. Be sure to ask about the free delivery of store purchases to the hotel.
> 64 blvd Haussmann, 9ᵉ
TEL 01 42 825 000
HOURS: 9:30 A.M. TO 7 P.M. MON TO SAT; UNTIL 10 P.M. ON THU
http://departmentstoreparis.printemps.com (The French version has more store locations listed).

Le Bon Marché is the oldest and most sumptuous department store in Paris. Open since 1848, everything, from shoes to tableware to toys, can be found under one roof. It stocks just about every famous designer, covering the needs of the whole family. It's now owned by the Big

Kahuna of powerhouse labels, *Louis Vuitton Moet Hennessy (LVMH),* so expect quality. There is a great restroom in the kids' department, complete with a changing table, water cooler, and a chair for nursing mothers. **Big plus:** on the third floor there are dressing rooms with phones to call a salesperson to request a different size. It is also one of the best toy stores in Paris, and just about every toy can be found here, from puzzles to fancy (expensive) costumes, equipped with wigs, and much more.
> 22 rue de Sèvres, 7ᵉ
TEL: 01 44 398 000
HOURS: 9:30 A.M. TO 7 P.M. MON TO WED; 10 A.M. TO 9 P.M. THU; 9:30 A.M. TO 7 P.M. FRI; SAT: 9:30 A.M. TO 8 P.M. SAT
www.bonmarche.fr

Play as you go: In front of the Le Bon Marché department store is Square Boucicaut, a small, good playground with a carousel, jungle gym and slide. It's a great place to run off some kid-energy before shopping, or use it to bribe the kids to be on their best behavior for a treat afterward.

Monoprix is the French equivalent of Target. Try the several branches of this reasonably priced department store located around the city (there are many more all over France). It is a hunting ground for cheap-chic parents.

This place also offers everything from cosmetics to housewares and bedding. The shops aren't as grand in size as Target stores, but the deals to be found—with a little added French flare—are quite similar. Some locations also have grocery stores.

> 52 av des Champs-Elysées, 8ᵉ
TEL: 01 53 776 565
www.monoprix.fr (for other locations)

SHOES

Remember those Camper shoes... mentioned earlier? The best ones for walking around Paris? Well, this is where you can find them—at 14 different locations in Paris! They're stylish, they're comfortable, they're a mother's dream. According to Camper's Web site, these shoes reflect "a new lifestyle, a new concept based on freedom, comfort and creativity." So strap on a pair and get walking. Among other outlets (listed on the Web site), the shoes can be found at *Shoe Bizz stores.*

> *Shoe Bizz*, 48 rue Beaubourg, 3ᵉ
TEL: 01 48 871 273
> *Shoe Bizz*, 42 rue Dragon, 6ᵉ
TEL 01 45 449 170
www.camper.com (for outlets)
Six Pieds Trois Pouces: Lovely and adorable fashionable Italian footwear for children.
> 223 blvd St.-Germain, 7ᵉ
TEL: 01 45 440 372
www.6pieds3pouces.com

WORTH A VISIT

Perfume: *Annick Goutal* is known throughout the world for its perfume. The *Eau de Bonpoint* fragrance for children and babies is always a treasured gift, and yes, it shares the same name as the prestigious children's clothing brand—so you know to expect quality. Older gals will love both Annick Goutal stores, which have been referred to as "jewel boxes".
> 14 rue de Castiglione, 1ᵉ
TEL: 01 42 605 282
> 12 place St. Sulpice, 6ᵉ
TEL: 01 46 330 315

Haircuts: *Bonton* offers reasonably priced haircuts for children. It is also a place to purchase chic baby gifts. It is a regular haunt of Catherine Deneuve's daughter, actress Chiar Mastroianni. Don't let this stop you: gifts and chic items can be found for children up to age 10.
> 82 rue de Grenelle, 7ᵉ
TEL: 01 44 390 920

English Bookstores: The Red Wheelbarrow Bookstore is a adorable petite store that is surprisingly well-stocked with loads of English-language children's books. Many are signed by well-known American writers and illustrators that have visited Paris—it is almost a tradition.
> 22 rue de la St-Paul, 4ᵉ
MÉTRO: ST. PAUL
TEL: 01 48 04 75 08

Hours: 10 a.m. to 7 p.m. Mon to Sat;
2 p.m. to 6 p.m. Sun
www.theredwheelbarrow.com
>**Brentano's** has an extensive
selection of children's books and
travel maps and guides.
> 37 avenue de l'Opera, 2e
Métro: Pyramides or Opéra
Hours: 10 A.M. to 7 P.M. daily
Tel: 01 42 615 250

Toys R' Us: No explanation
needed. The kids know.
> Centre Commercial
Quatre-Temps, La Défense
Tel: 01 47 762 978
www.toysrus.fr

Gap: Over 10 locations
throughout the city, in various
sizes. The largest Gap
store location is on *Avenue
des Champs-Elysées.*
> 36 av des Champs-Elysées, 8ᵉ
Tel: 01 56 884 800
www.gapkids.com

MARKETS

Paris, like most major European
cities, is home to many outdoor
markets. Each neighborhood
usually has its weekly food
market, while other markets
offer a variety of items. The web
site of the *Mairie de Paris* has a
full list of markets by district.
Go to **www.v1.paris.fr/EN/** then
click on Markets in the list on the
right-hand side of the page. You
can then choose between general
markets and specialized markets.

Here are two favorites you don't
want to miss:

Flea Market
Marché aux Puces de St-Ouen:
This is the biggest, oldest and
certainly most famous flea market
in Paris, if not Europe. You'll find
everything imaginable, from
antiques to toy animals here.
Situated in the northern outskirts
of the city, be sure to include time
in your visit for a good 10-15 minute
walk from the *Clignancourt métro*
stop. Sadly, the area around the
Clignancourt métro stop is not
a stroller-friendly environment
for young children. New stock
generally arrives to the market on
Friday, and it's generally known as
the day the professionals tend to
shop. Some stalls will take credit
cards, and be sure to bargain for
just about everything.
> Rue des Rosiers, St-Ouen, 18ᵉ
Métro: Porte de Clignancourt,
Hours: 7am-6pm Sat to Mon

Flower and Bird Market
Since 1808, *Place Louis Lépine* has
been the home of the year-round
Marché aux Fleurs, the oldest and
one of the largest flower markets
in Paris. On Sundays, it also hosts
the ***Marché aux Oiseaux*** bird
market. Take a walk around, and let
your children enjoy the birds, color
and atmosphere.
> Place Louis Lépine, 14ᵉ
Métro: Cité
Hours: 8 a.m. to 7 p.m.

INDEX

Paris * BY TABLE OF CONTENTS

Climbing the Eiffel Tower   105

Paris * IN ALPHABETICAL ORDER